HARLEQUIN VALENTINE™

Neil Gaiman
WRITER

John Bolton
ARTIST

For Lisa Snellings

Diana Schutz
EDITOR

Cary Grazzini
BOOK DESIGN

Richard Starkings &
Comicraft's Jason Levine
LETTERING

Mike Richardson
PUBLISHER

Published by
Dark Horse Comics, Inc.
10956 SE Main Street
Milwaukie, Oregon 97222

First edition: November 2001
ISBN 1-56971-620-6

PRINTED IN SINGAPORE

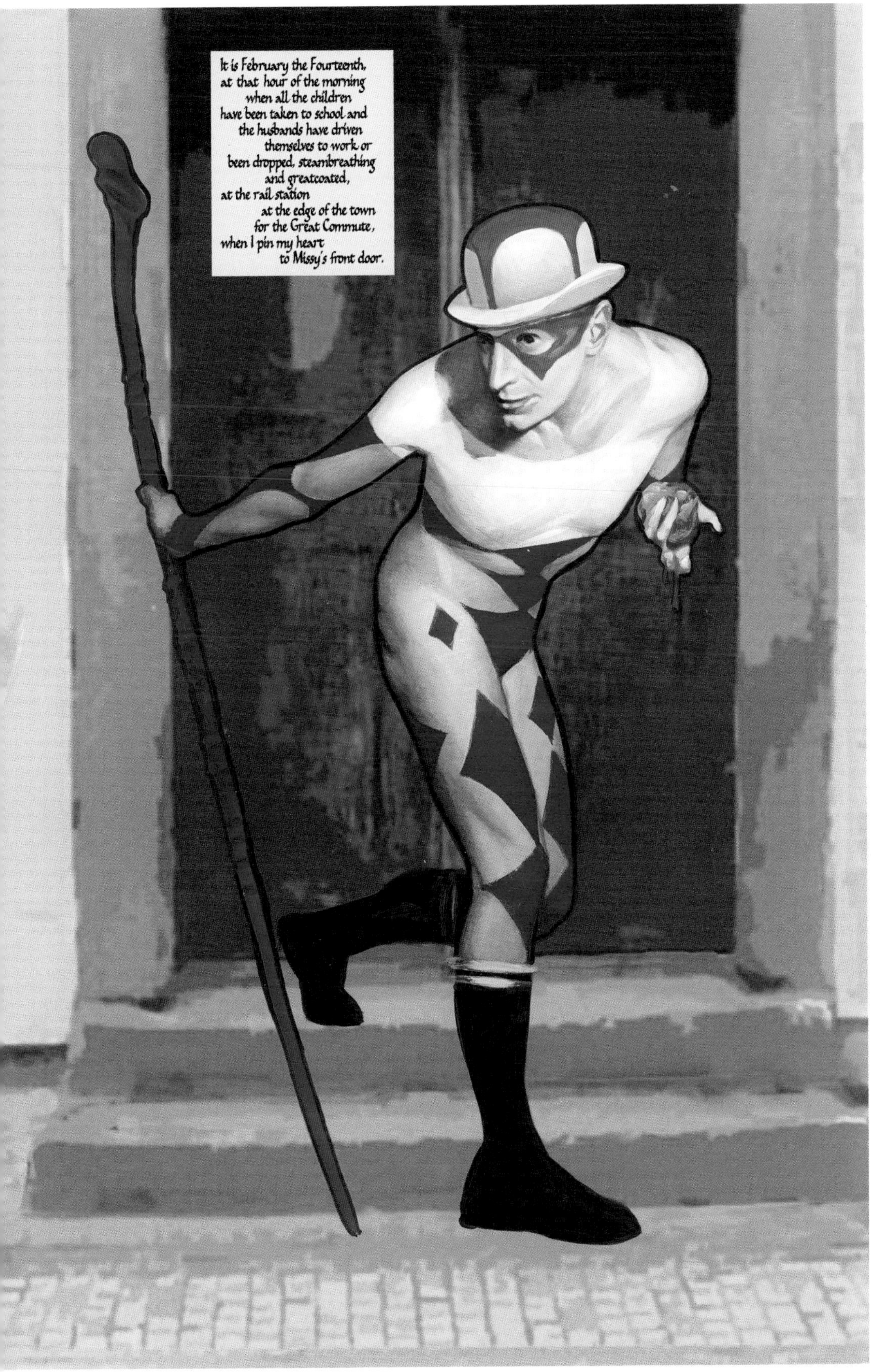
It is February the Fourteenth,
at that hour of the morning
when all the children
have been taken to school and
the husbands have driven
themselves to work or
been dropped, steambreathing
and greatcoated,
at the rail station
at the edge of the town
for the Great Commute,
when I pin my heart
to Missy's front door.

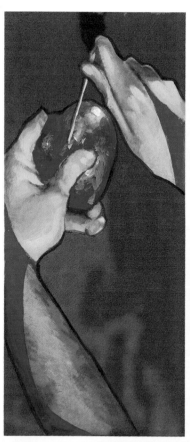

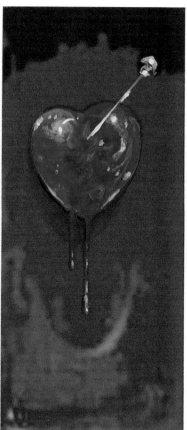

The heart is a deep dark red that is almost a brown, the colour of liver.

Then I knock on the door, sharply, rat-a-tat-tat!

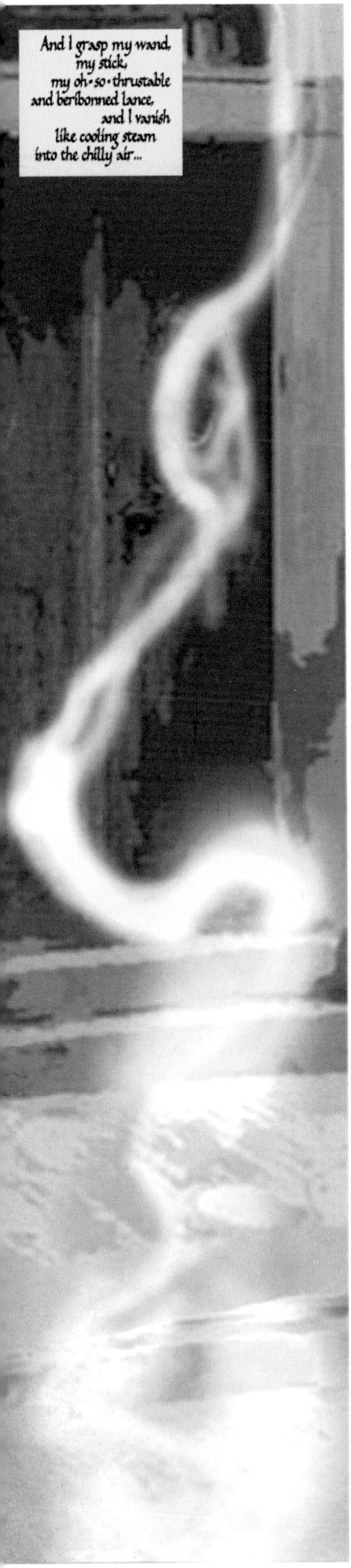
And I grasp my wand,
my stick,
my oh-so-thrustable
and beribboned lance,
and I vanish
like cooling steam
into the chilly air...

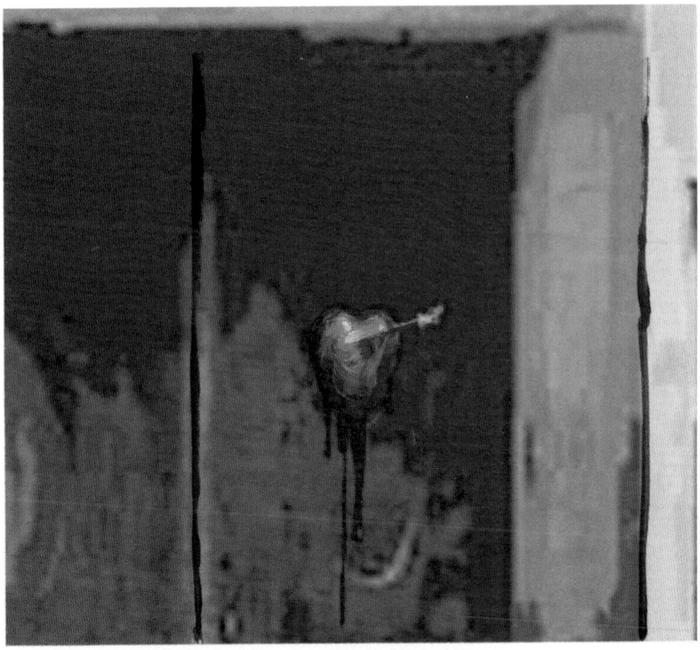

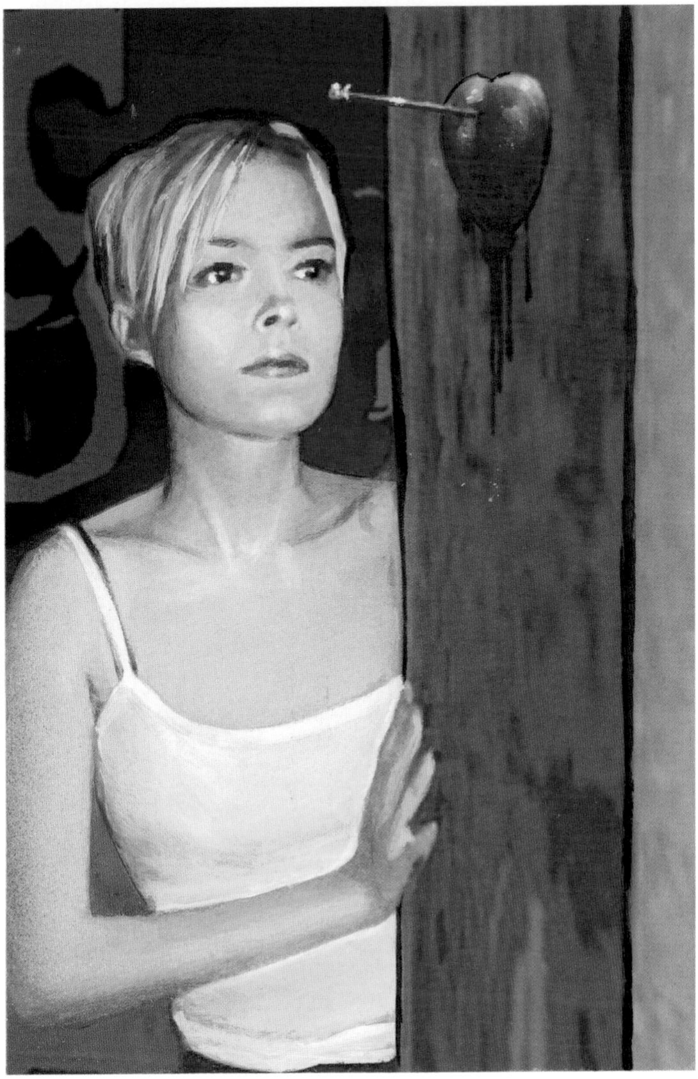

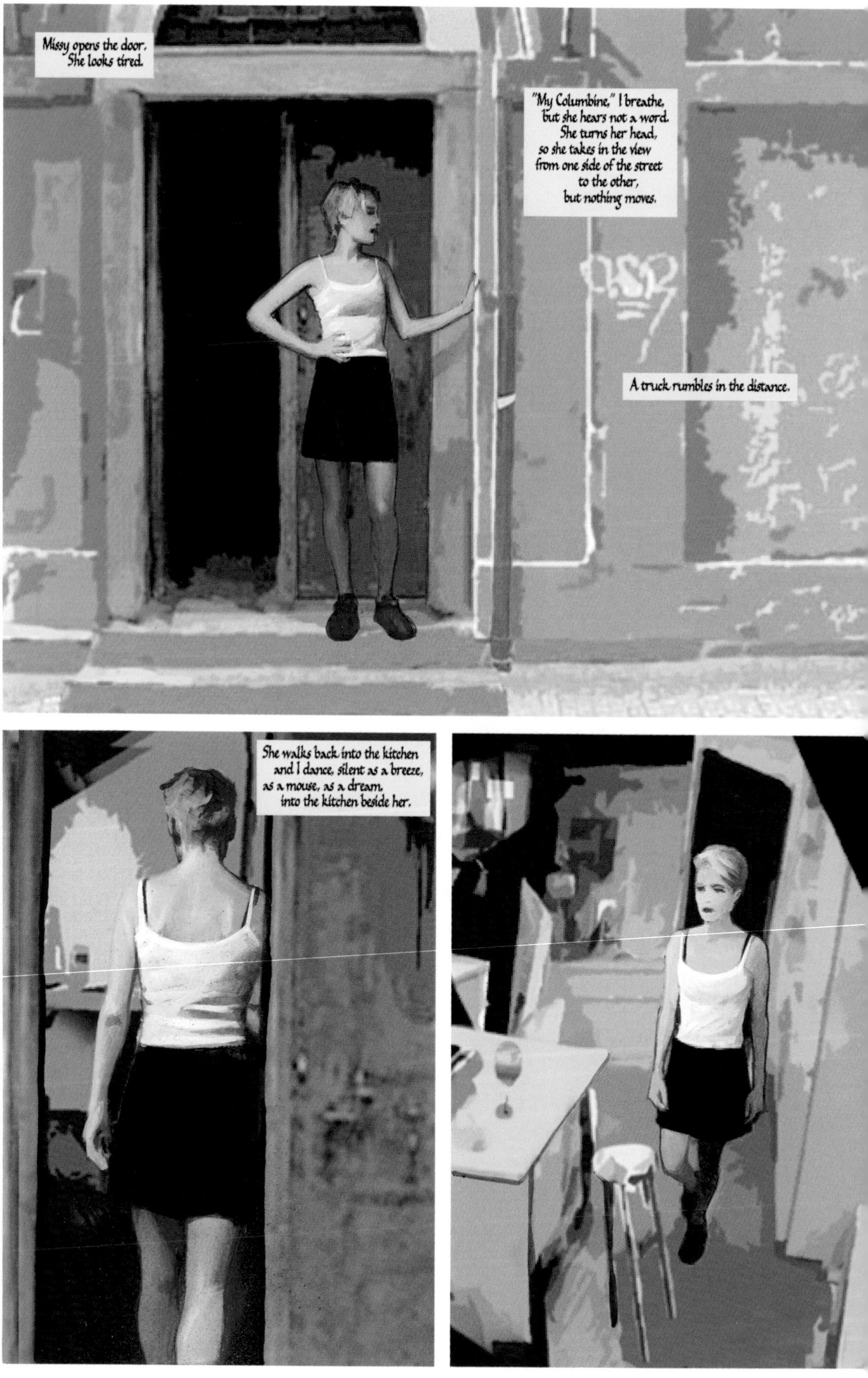
Missy opens the door. She looks tired.
"My Columbine," I breathe, but she hears not a word. She turns her head, so she takes in the view from one side of the street to the other, but nothing moves.
A truck rumbles in the distance.
She walks back into the kitchen and I dance, silent as a breeze, as a mouse, as a dream, into the kitchen beside her.

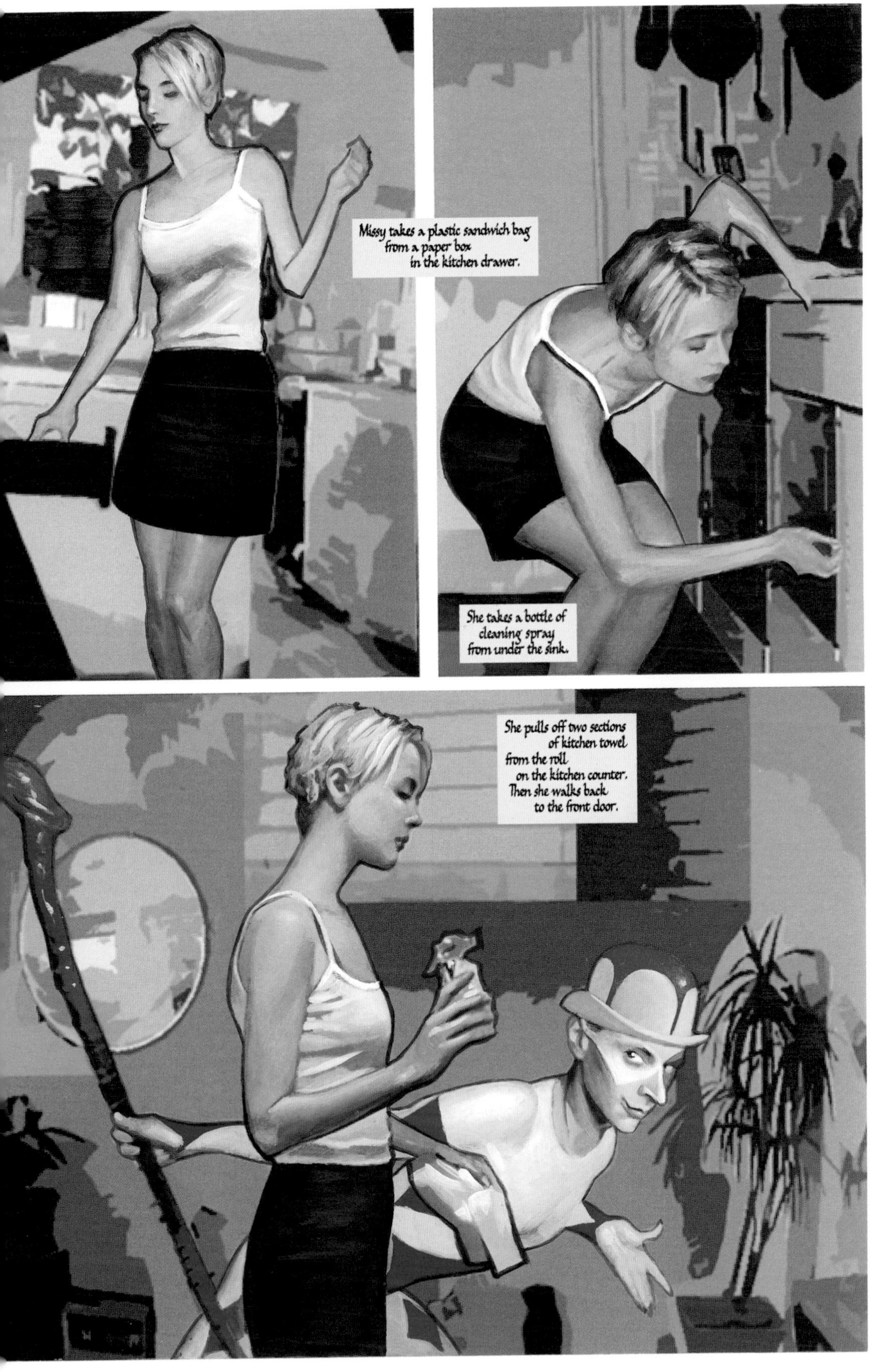
Missy takes a plastic sandwich bag
from a paper box
in the kitchen drawer.
She takes a bottle of
cleaning spray
from under the sink.
She pulls off two sections
of kitchen towel
from the roll
on the kitchen counter.
Then she walks back
to the front door.

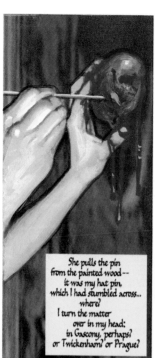

She pulls the pin
from the painted wood --
it was my hat pin,
which I had stumbled across...
where?
I turn the matter
over in my head:
in Gascony, perhaps?
or Twickenham? or Prague?

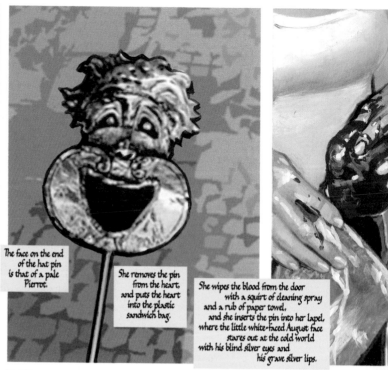

The face on the end
of the hat pin
is that of a pale
Pierrot.

She removes the pin
from the heart,
and puts the heart
into the plastic
sandwich bag.

She wipes the blood from the door
with a squirt of cleaning spray
and a rub of paper towel,
and she inserts the pin into her lapel,
where the little white-faced August face
stares out at the cold world
with his blind silver eyes and
his grave silver lips.

Naples. Now it comes back to me.

I purchased the hat pin
in Naples,
from an old woman
with one eye.
She smoked a clay pipe.
This was a long time ago.

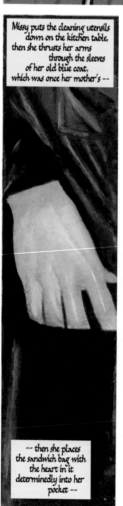

Missy puts the cleaning utensils
down on the kitchen table,
then she thrusts her arms
through the sleeves
of her old blue coat,
which was once her mother's --

-- then she places
the sandwich bag with
the heart in it
determinedly into her
pocket --

-- does up
the buttons,
one,
two,
three --

-- and sets off
down the street.

8

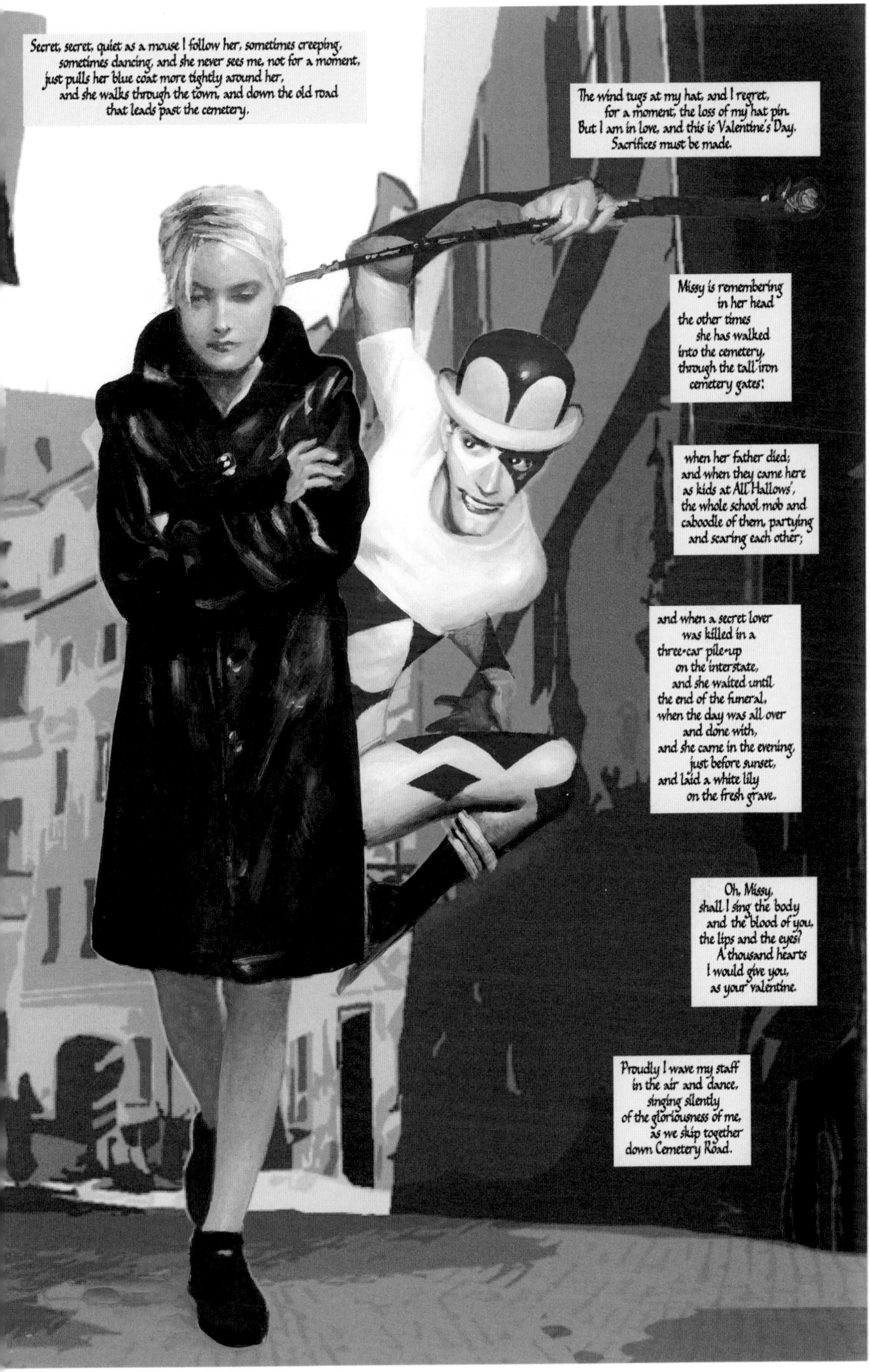
Secret, secret, quiet as a mouse I follow her, sometimes creeping, sometimes dancing, and she never sees me, not for a moment, just pulls her blue coat more tightly around her, and she walks through the town, and down the old road that leads past the cemetery.
The wind tugs at my hat, and I regret, for a moment, the loss of my hat pin. But I am in love, and this is Valentine's Day. Sacrifices must be made.
Missy is remembering in her head the other times she has walked into the cemetery, through the tall iron cemetery gates:
when her father died; and when they came here as kids at All Hallows', the whole school mob and caboodle of them, partying and scaring each other;
and when a secret lover was killed in a three-car pile-up on the interstate, and she waited until the end of the funeral, when the day was all over and done with, and she came in the evening, just before sunset, and laid a white lily on the fresh grave.
Oh, Missy, shall I sing the body and the blood of you, the lips and the eyes? A thousand hearts I would give you, as your valentine.
Proudly I wave my staff in the air and dance, singing silently of the gloriousness of me, as we skip together down Cemetery Road.

A low grey building, and Missy pushes open the door.

She says *Hi* and *How's it going* to the girl at the desk, who makes no intelligible reply, fresh out of school and filling in a crossword from a periodical filled with nothing but crosswords, page after page of them...

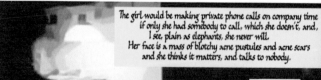

The girl would be making private phone calls on company time if only she had somebody to call, which she doesn't, and, I see, plain as elephants, she never will. Her face is a mass of blotchy acne pustules and acne scars and she thinks it matters, and talks to nobody.

I see her life spread out before me:

She will die, unmarried, and unmolested, of breast cancer in fifteen years' time, and will be planted under a stone with her name on it in the meadow by Cemetery Road, and the first hands to have touched her breasts will have been those of the pathologist as he cuts out the cauliflower-like stinking growth and mutters,

JESUS, LOOK AT THE *SIZE* OF THIS THING. WHY DIDN'T SHE *TELL* ANYONE?

which rather misses the point.

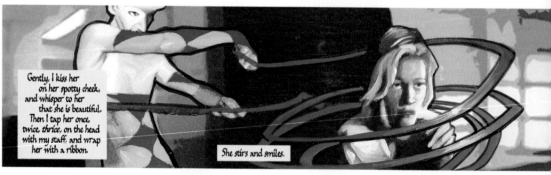

Gently, I kiss her on her spotty cheek, and whisper to her that she is beautiful. Then I tap her once, twice, *thrice*, on the head with my staff, and wrap her with a ribbon.

She stirs and smiles.

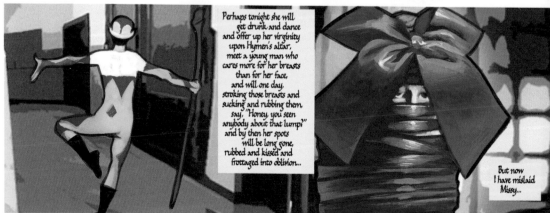

Perhaps tonight she will get drunk and dance and offer up her virginity upon Hymen's altar, meet a young man who cares more for her breasts than for her face, and will one day, stroking those breasts and sucking and rubbing them, say, "Honey, you seen anybody about that lump?" and by then her spots will be long gone, rubbed and kissed and frottaged into oblivion...

But now I have mislaid Missy...

10

The stench is unbelievable, heavy and rancid and wretched on the air. The fat man in the stained lab coat wears disposable rubber gloves. A dead man is on the table in front of him.

The fat man has not noticed Missy yet. He has made an incision, and now he peels back the skin with a wet, sucking sound, and how dark the brown of it is on the outside, and how pink, pretty the pink of it is on the inside.

Classical music plays from a portable radio, very loudly.

Missy turns the radio off.

HELLO, VERNON.

HELLO, MISSY. YOU COME FOR YOUR OLD JOB BACK?

This is The Doctor, I decide, for he is too big, too round, too magnificently well-fed to be Pierrot, too unselfconscious to be Pantaloon.

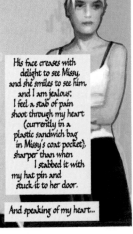

His face creases with delight to see Missy, and she smiles to see him, and I am jealous: I feel a stab of pain shoot through my heart (currently in a plastic sandwich bag in Missy's coat pocket), sharper than when I stabbed it with my hat pin and stuck it to her door.

And speaking of my heart...

DO YOU KNOW WHAT *THIS* IS?

HEART. KIDNEYS DON'T HAVE THE VENTRICLES, AND BRAINS ARE BIGGER AND SQUISHIER. WHERE'D YOU *GET* IT?

I WAS HOPING THAT *YOU* COULD TELL *ME.* DOESN'T IT COME FROM HERE? IS IT YOUR IDEA OF A VALENTINE'S CARD, VERNON? A HUMAN HEART STUCK TO MY FRONT DOOR?

DON'T COME FROM HERE. YOU WANT I SHOULD CALL THE POLICE?

I GUESS *NOT*. WITH *MY* LUCK, THEY'LL DECIDE I'M A SERIAL KILLER AND SEND ME TO THE CHAIR.

LET'S *SEE...* ADULT, IN PRETTY GOOD SHAPE, TOOK CARE OF HIS HEART. CUT OUT BY AN EXPERT.

I smile proudly at this, and bend down to talk to the dead black man on the table, with his chest all open and his calloused string-bass-picking fingers.

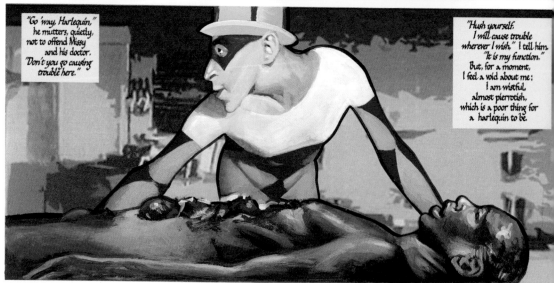

"Go 'way, Harlequin," he mutters, quietly, not to offend Missy and his doctor. *"Don't you go causing trouble here."*

"Hush yourself. I will cause trouble wherever I wish," I tell him. *"It is my function."* But, for a moment, I feel a void about me: I am wistful, almost pierrotish, which is a poor thing for a harlequin to be.

Oh, Missy, I saw you yesterday in the street, and followed you into Al's Super-Valu Foods and More, elation and joy rising within me. In you, I recognised someone who could transport me, take me from myself.

In you I recognised my valentine.

My Columbine.

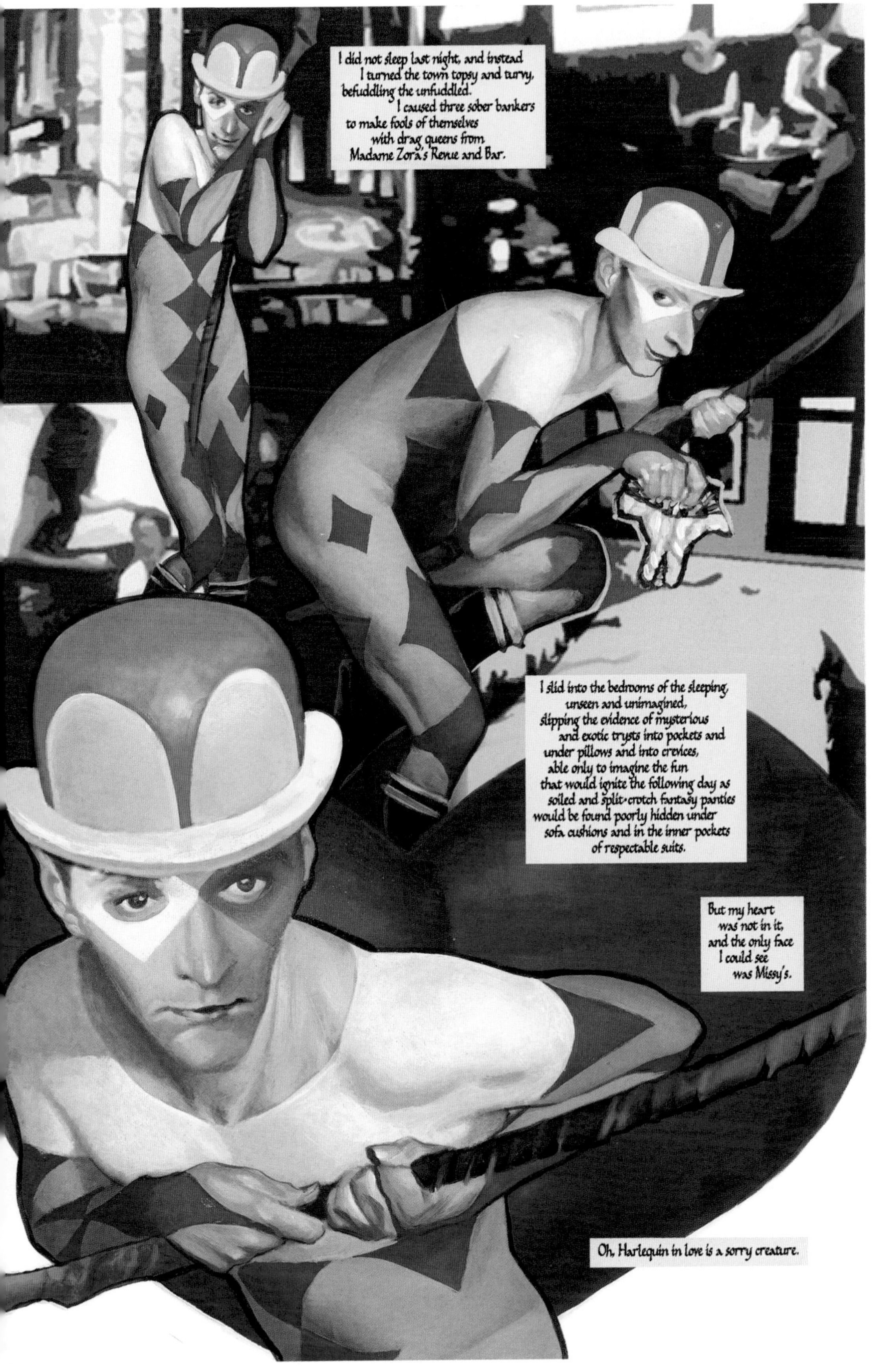
I did not sleep last night, and instead
I turned the town topsy and turvy,
befuddling the unfuddled.
I caused three sober bankers
to make fools of themselves
with drag queens from
Madame Zora's Revue and Bar.
I slid into the bedrooms of the sleeping,
unseen and unimagined,
slipping the evidence of mysterious
and exotic trysts into pockets and
under pillows and into crevices,
able only to imagine the fun
that would ignite the following day as
soiled and split-crotch fantasy panties
would be found poorly hidden under
sofa cushions and in the inner pockets
of respectable suits.
But my heart
was not in it,
and the only face
I could see
was Missy's.
Oh, Harlequin in love is a sorry creature.

I wonder what she will do with my gift.
Some girls spurn my heart,
others touch it, kiss it, caress it, punish it
with all manner of endearments before
they return it to my keeping.
Some never even see it...

SHALL I *INCINERATE* IT?

MIGHT AS WELL. YOU KNOW WHERE THE INCINERATOR IS. AND I MEANT WHAT I SAID ABOUT YOUR OLD JOB. I *NEED* A GOOD LAB ASSISTANT.

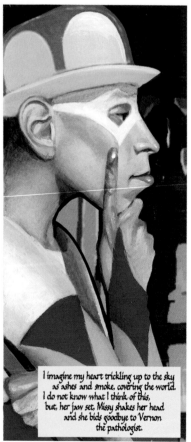

I imagine my heart trickling up to the sky
as ashes and smoke, covering the world.
I do not know what I think of this,
but, her jaw set, Missy shakes her head
and she bids goodbye to Vernon
the pathologist.

She has thrust my heart into her pocket and
she is walking out of the building and up
Cemetery Road and back into town.

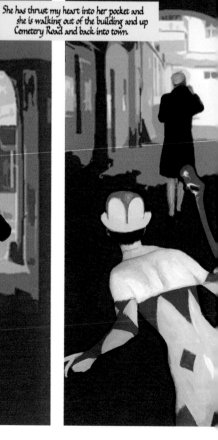

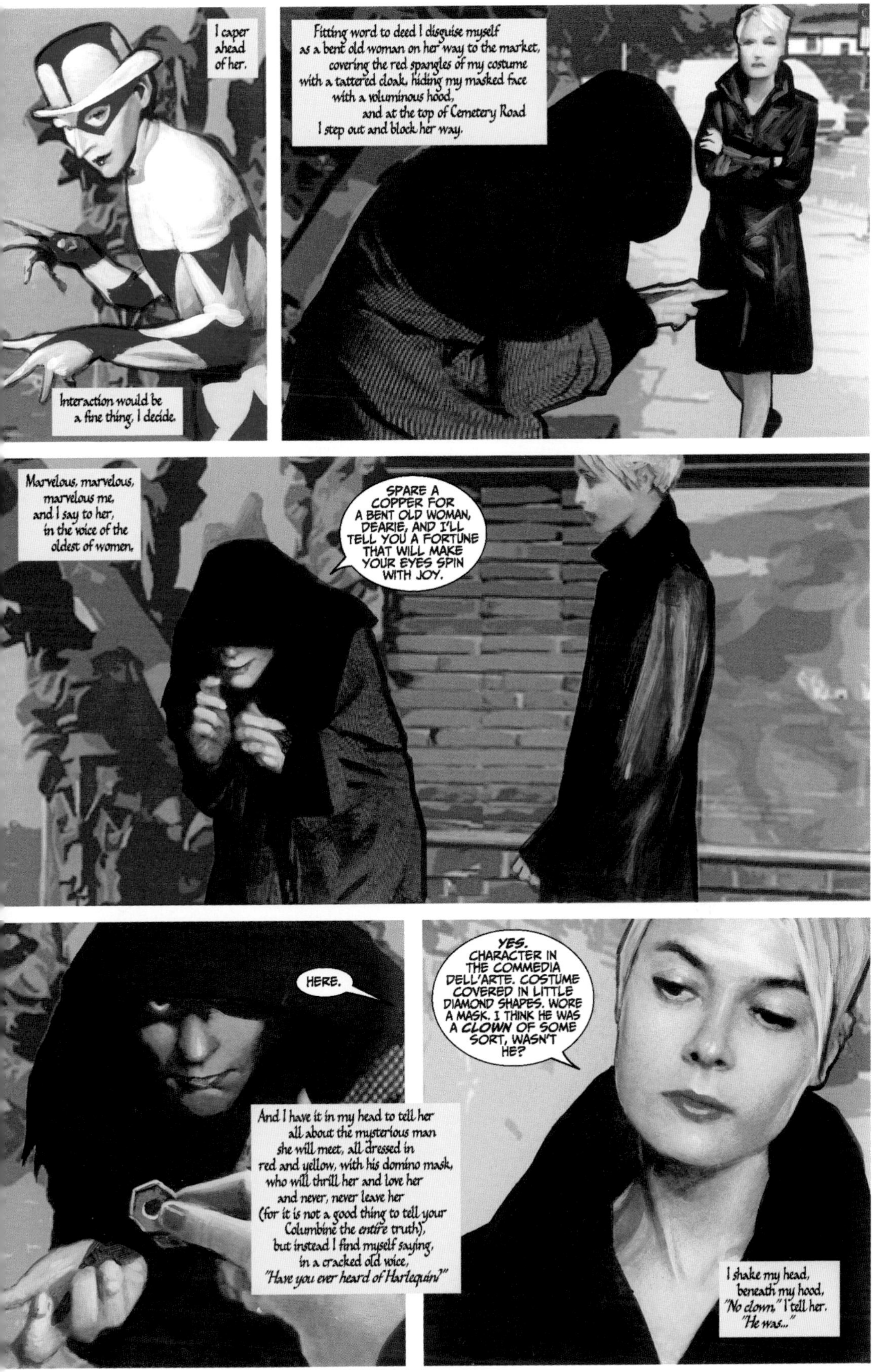
I caper ahead of her.
Interaction would be a fine thing, I decide.
Fitting word to deed I disguise myself as a bent old woman on her way to the market, covering the red spangles of my costume with a tattered cloak, hiding my masked face with a voluminous hood, and at the top of Cemetery Road I step out and block her way.
Marvelous, marvelous, marvelous me, and I say to her, in the voice of the oldest of women,
SPARE A COPPER FOR A BENT OLD WOMAN, DEARIE, AND I'LL TELL YOU A FORTUNE THAT WILL MAKE YOUR EYES SPIN WITH JOY.
HERE.
And I have it in my head to tell her all about the mysterious man she will meet, all dressed in red and yellow, with his domino mask, who will thrill her and love her and never, never leave her (for it is not a good thing to tell your Columbine the *entire* truth), but instead I find myself saying, in a cracked old voice, *"Have you ever heard of Harlequin?"*
YES. CHARACTER IN THE COMMEDIA DELL'ARTE. COSTUME COVERED IN LITTLE DIAMOND SHAPES. WORE A MASK. I THINK HE WAS A *CLOWN* OF SOME SORT, WASN'T HE?
I shake my head, beneath my hood. *"No clown,"* I tell her. *"He was..."*

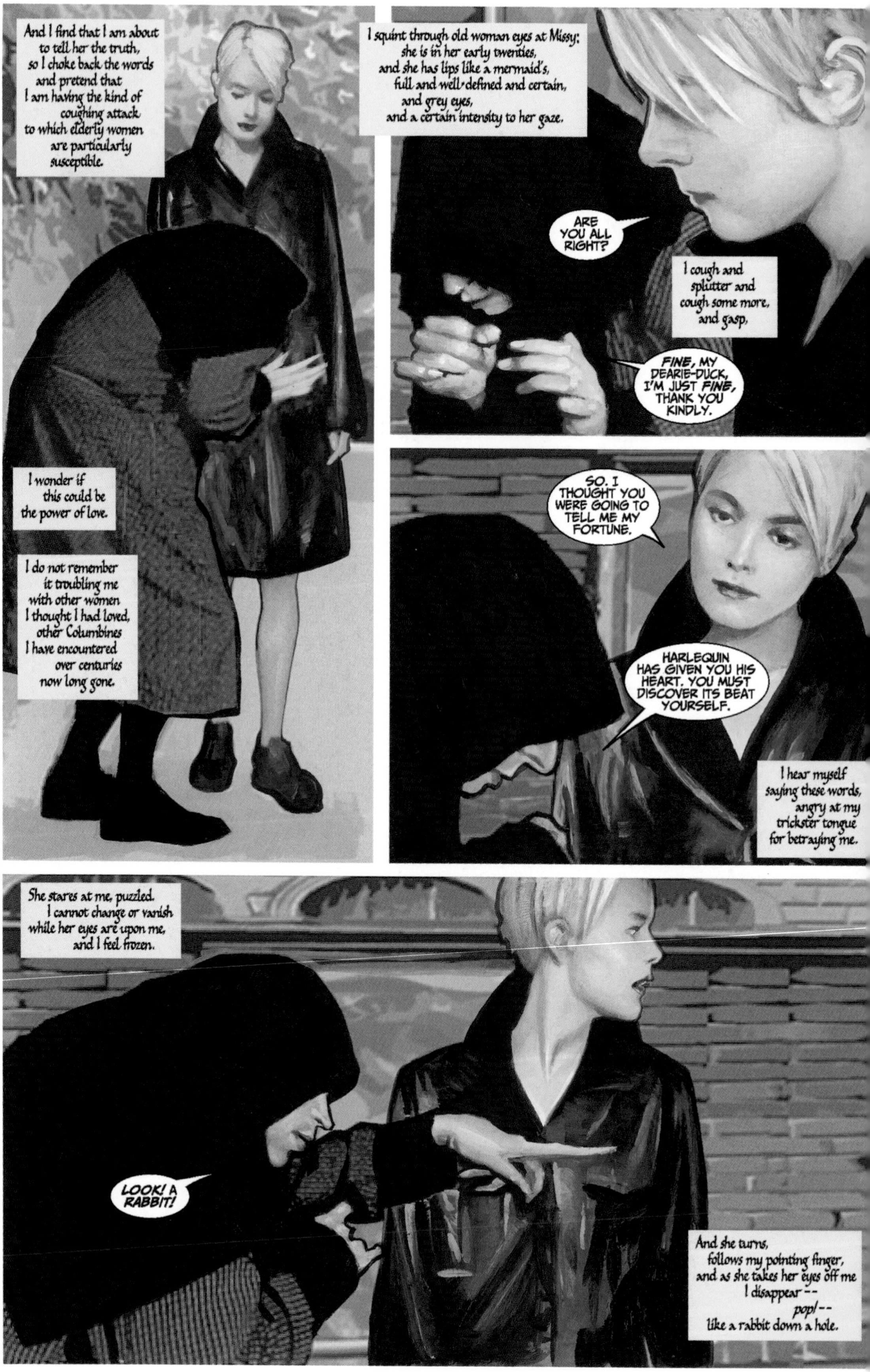
And I find that I am about to tell her the truth, so I choke back the words and pretend that I am having the kind of coughing attack to which elderly women are particularly susceptible.
I wonder if this could be the power of love.
I do not remember it troubling me with other women I thought I had loved, other Columbines I have encountered over centuries now long gone.
I squint through old woman eyes at Missy: she is in her early twenties, and she has lips like a mermaid's, full and well-defined and certain, and grey eyes, and a certain intensity to her gaze.
ARE YOU ALL RIGHT?
I cough and splutter and cough some more, and gasp,
FINE, MY DEARIE-DUCK, I'M JUST FINE, THANK YOU KINDLY.
SO. I THOUGHT YOU WERE GOING TO TELL ME MY FORTUNE.
HARLEQUIN HAS GIVEN YOU HIS HEART. YOU MUST DISCOVER ITS BEAT YOURSELF.
I hear myself saying these words, angry at my trickster tongue for betraying me.
She stares at me, puzzled. I cannot change or vanish while her eyes are upon me, and I feel frozen.
LOOK! A RABBIT!
And she turns, follows my pointing finger, and as she takes her eyes off me I disappear -- pop! -- like a rabbit down a hole.

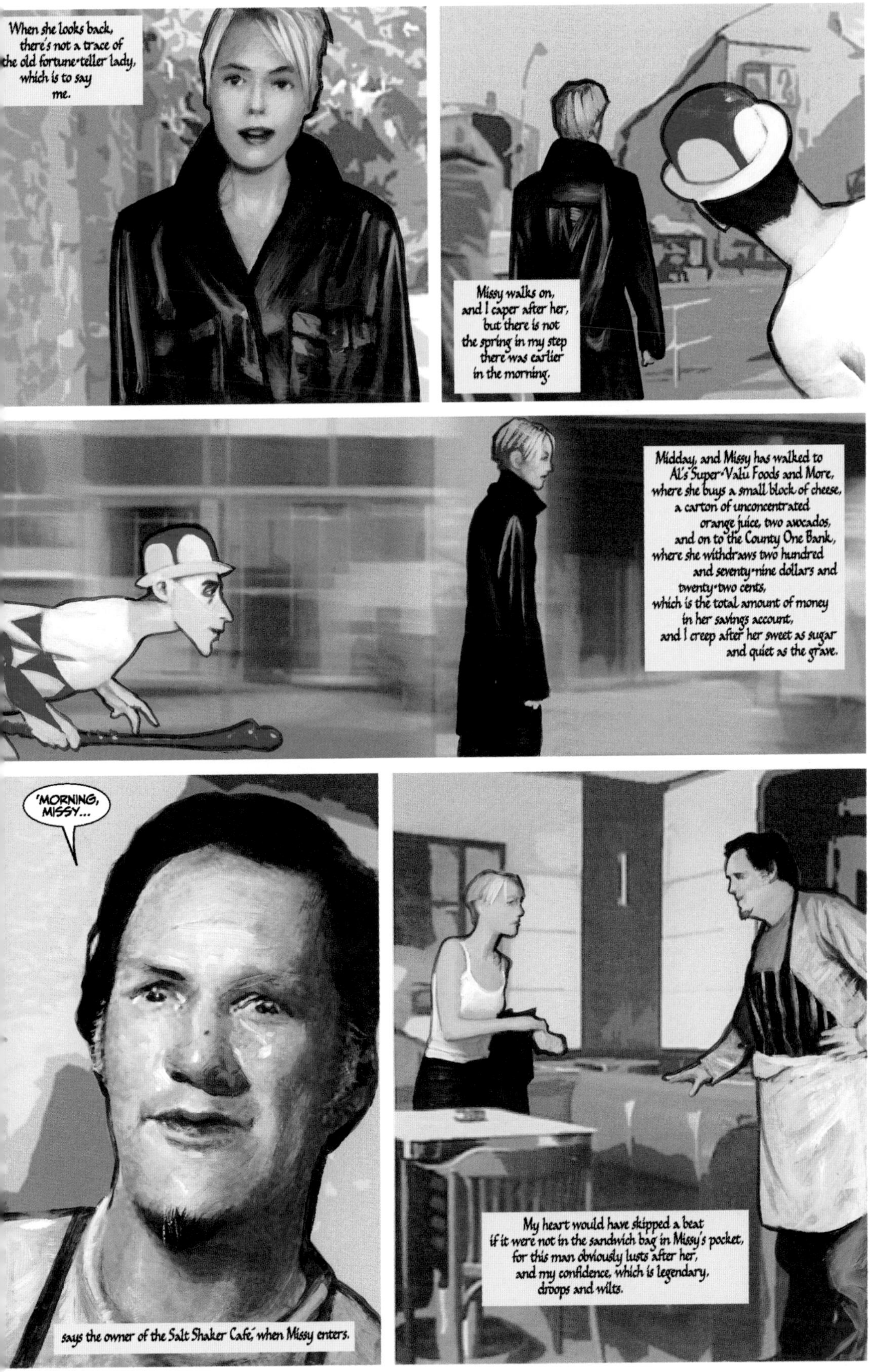
When she looks back, there's not a trace of the old fortune-teller lady, which is to say me.
Missy walks on, and I caper after her, but there is not the spring in my step there was earlier in the morning.
Midday, and Missy has walked to Al's Super-Valu Foods and More, where she buys a small block of cheese, a carton of unconcentrated orange juice, two avocados, and on to the County One Bank, where she withdraws two hundred and seventy-nine dollars and twenty-two cents, which is the total amount of money in her savings account, and I creep after her sweet as sugar and quiet as the grave.
'MORNING, MISSY...
says the owner of the Salt Shaker Café when Missy enters.
My heart would have skipped a beat if it were not in the sandwich bag in Missy's pocket, for this man obviously lusts after her, and my confidence, which is legendary, droops and wilts.

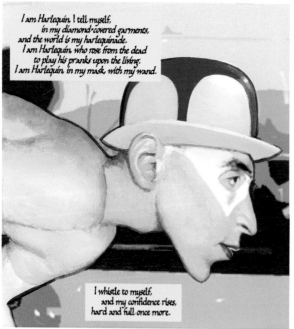

I am Harlequin, I tell myself,
in my diamond-covered garments,
and the world is my harlequinade.
I am Harlequin who rose from the dead
to play his pranks upon the living.
I am Harlequin in my mask, with my wand.

I whistle to myself,
and my confidence rises,
hard and full once more.

HEY, HARVE.
GIVE ME A PLATE
OF HASH BROWNS,
AND A BOTTLE
OF KETCHUP.

THAT
ALL?

YES.
THAT'LL BE
PERFECT. AND
A GLASS OF
WATER.

I tell myself that the man Harve
is Pantaloon,
the foolish merchant that I must
bamboozle, baffle, confusticate,
and confuse.

Perhaps there is
a string of sausages
in the kitchen.

I resolve to bring
delightful disarray
to the world, and
to bed luscious Missy
before midnight;
my Valentine's present
to myself.

I imagine myself kissing her lips.

There are a handful of other diners.
I amuse myself by swapping their plates
while they are not looking,
but I have difficulty finding the fun in it.

The waitress ignores Missy,
whom she obviously
considers entirely
Harve's preserve.

18

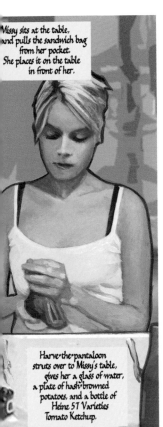

Missy sits at the table, and pulls the sandwich bag from her pocket. She places it on the table in front of her.

Harve-the-pantaloon struts over to Missy's table, gives her a glass of water, a plate of hash-browned potatoes, and a bottle of Heinz 57 Varieties Tomato Ketchup.

AND A STEAK KNIFE.

He curses, and I feel better, more like the former me.

I goose the waitress as she passes the table of an old man who is reading *USA Today* while toying with his salad.

She gives the old man a filthy look. I chuckle, and then I find I am feeling most peculiar.

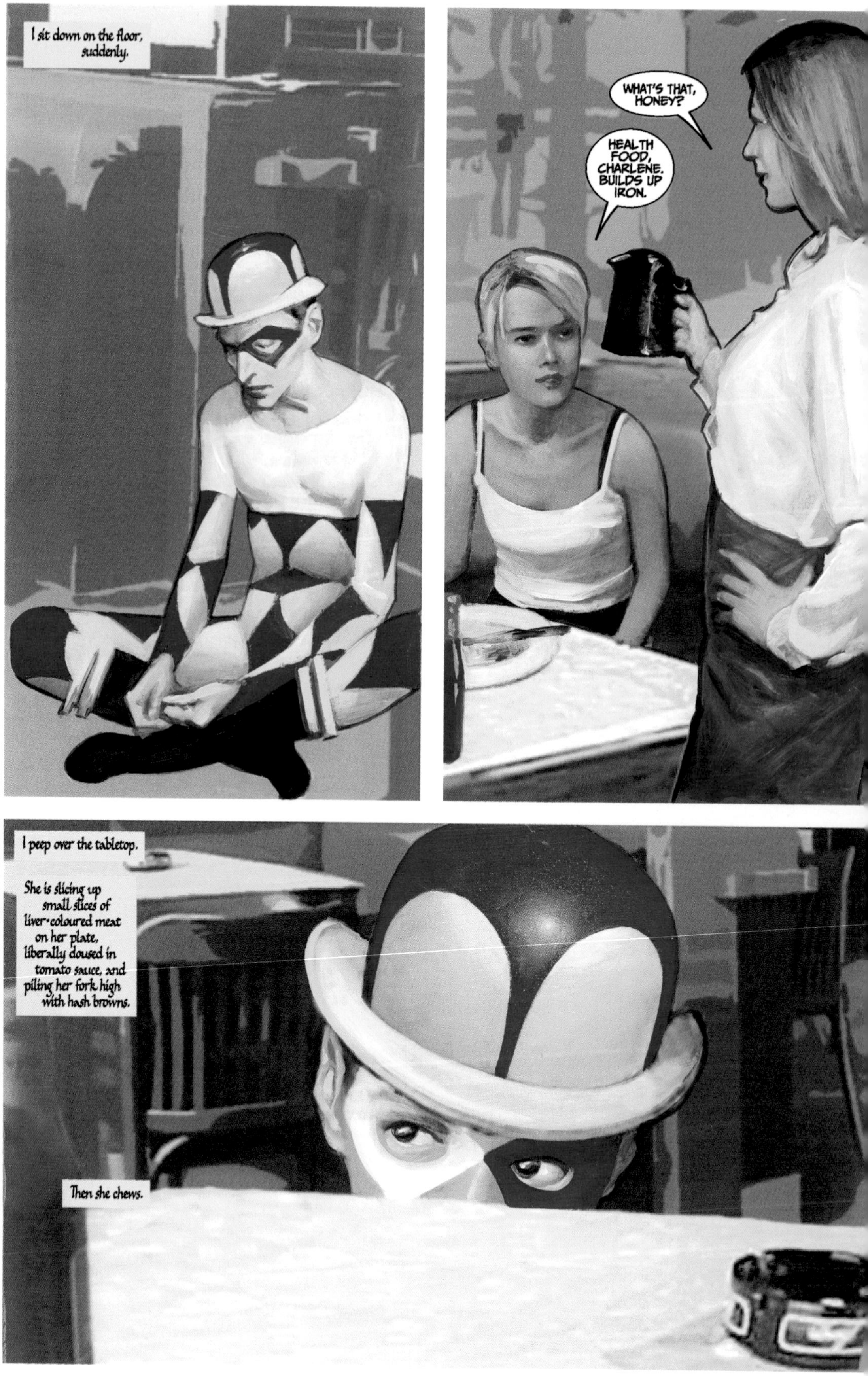

I sit down on the floor, suddenly.
WHAT'S THAT, HONEY?
HEALTH FOOD, CHARLENE. BUILDS UP IRON.
I peep over the tabletop.
She is slicing up small slices of liver-coloured meat on her plate, liberally doused in tomato sauce, and piling her fork high with hash browns.
Then she chews.

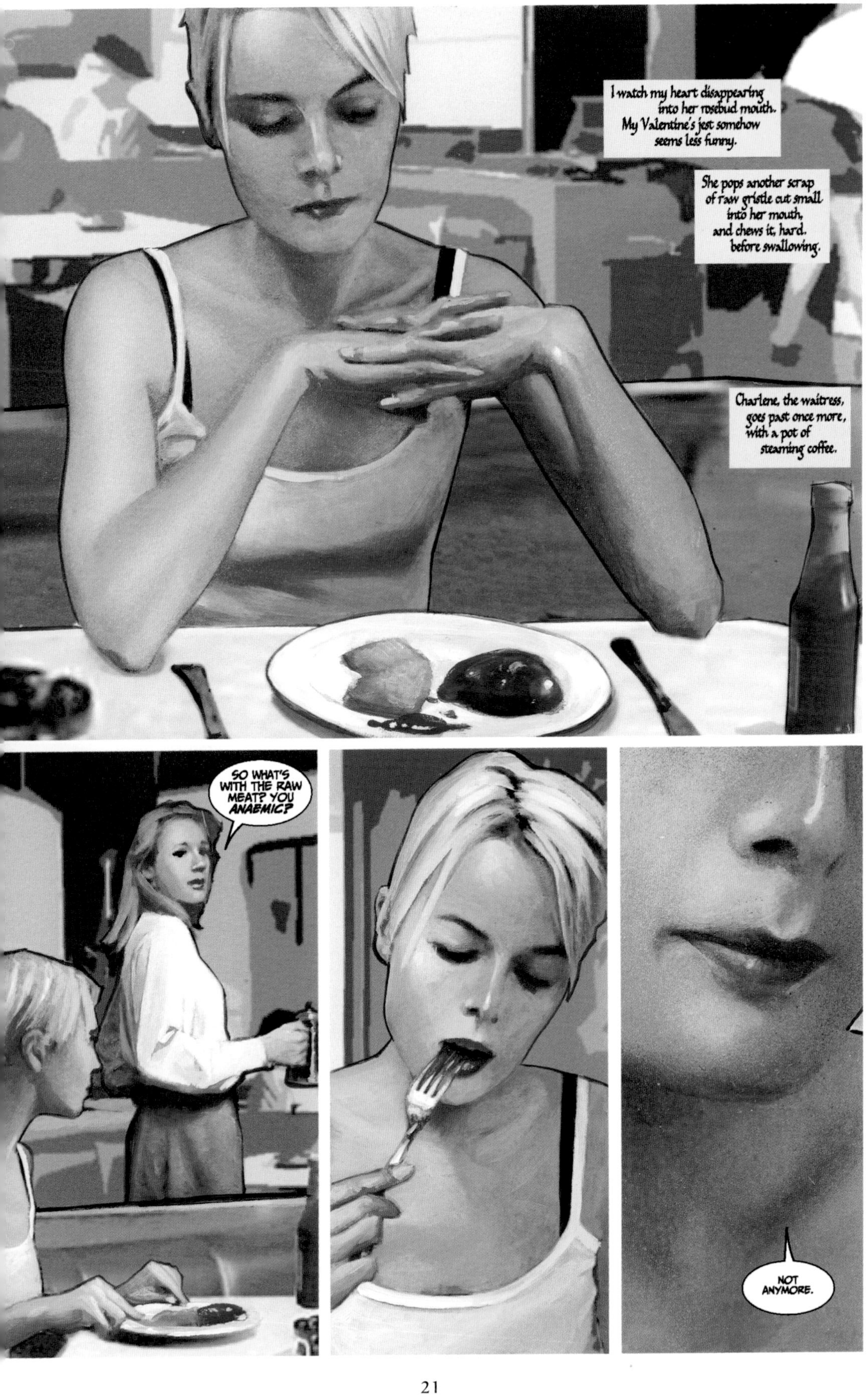
I watch my heart disappearing into her rosebud mouth. My Valentine's jest somehow seems less funny.
She pops another scrap of raw gristle cut small into her mouth, and chews it, hard. before swallowing.
Charlene, the waitress, goes past once more, with a pot of steaming coffee.
SO WHAT'S WITH THE RAW MEAT? YOU ANAEMIC?
NOT ANYMORE.

And as she finishes eating my heart, Missy looks down and sees me sprawled upon the floor. She nods.

OUTSIDE. NOW.

Then she gets up, and leaves ten dollars beside her plate.

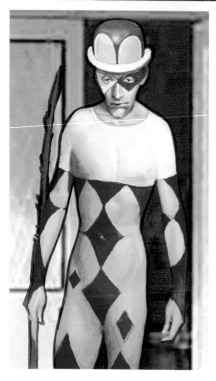

She is sitting on a bench on the sidewalk, waiting for me. It is cold, and the street is almost deserted.

I would caper around her, but it feels so foolish now I know someone is watching.

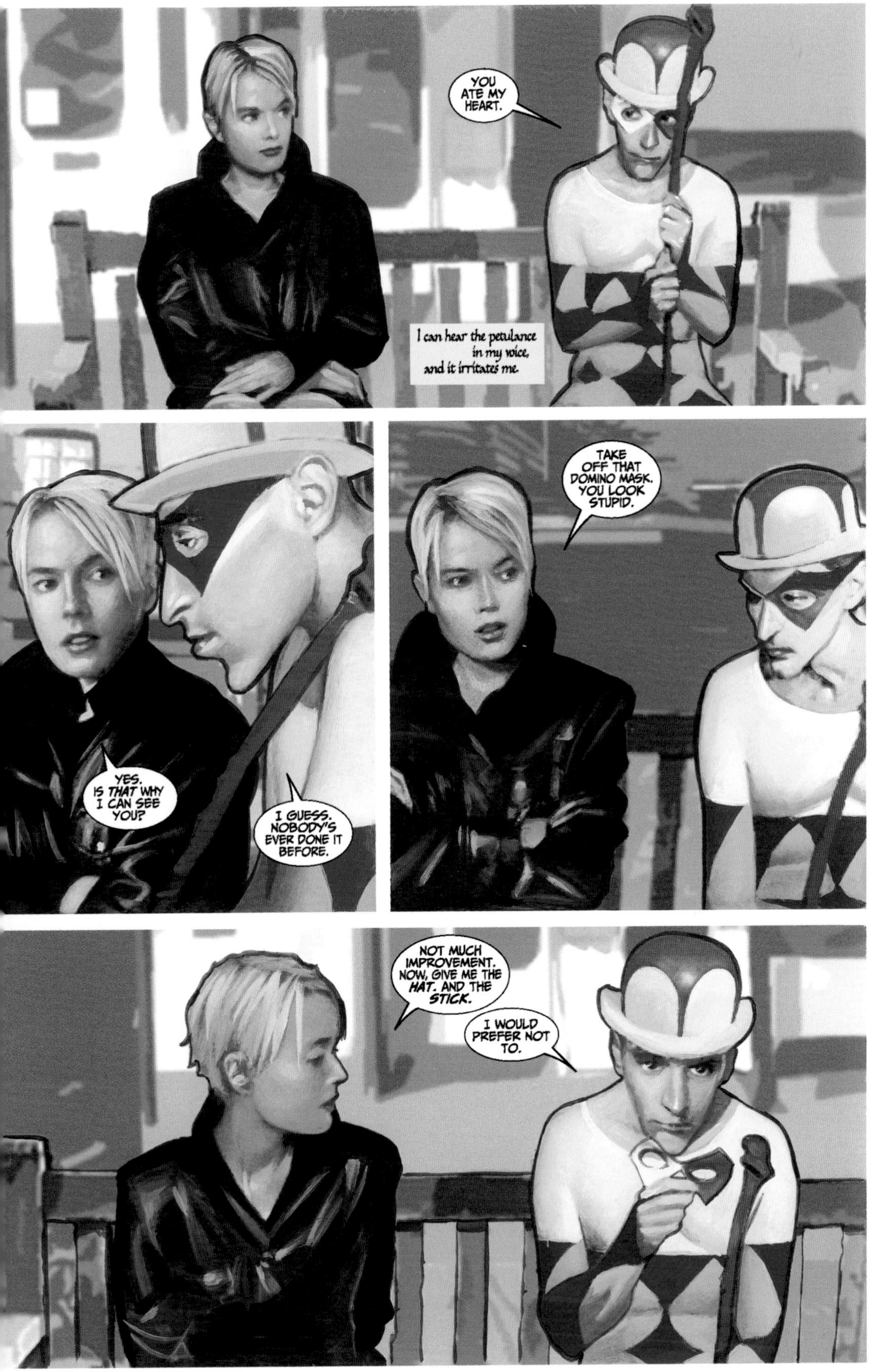
YOU ATE MY HEART.
I can hear the petulance in my voice, and it irritates me.
YES. IS THAT WHY I CAN SEE YOU?
I GUESS. NOBODY'S EVER DONE IT BEFORE.
TAKE OFF THAT DOMINO MASK. YOU LOOK STUPID.
NOT MUCH IMPROVEMENT. NOW, GIVE ME THE HAT. AND THE STICK.
I WOULD PREFER NOT TO.

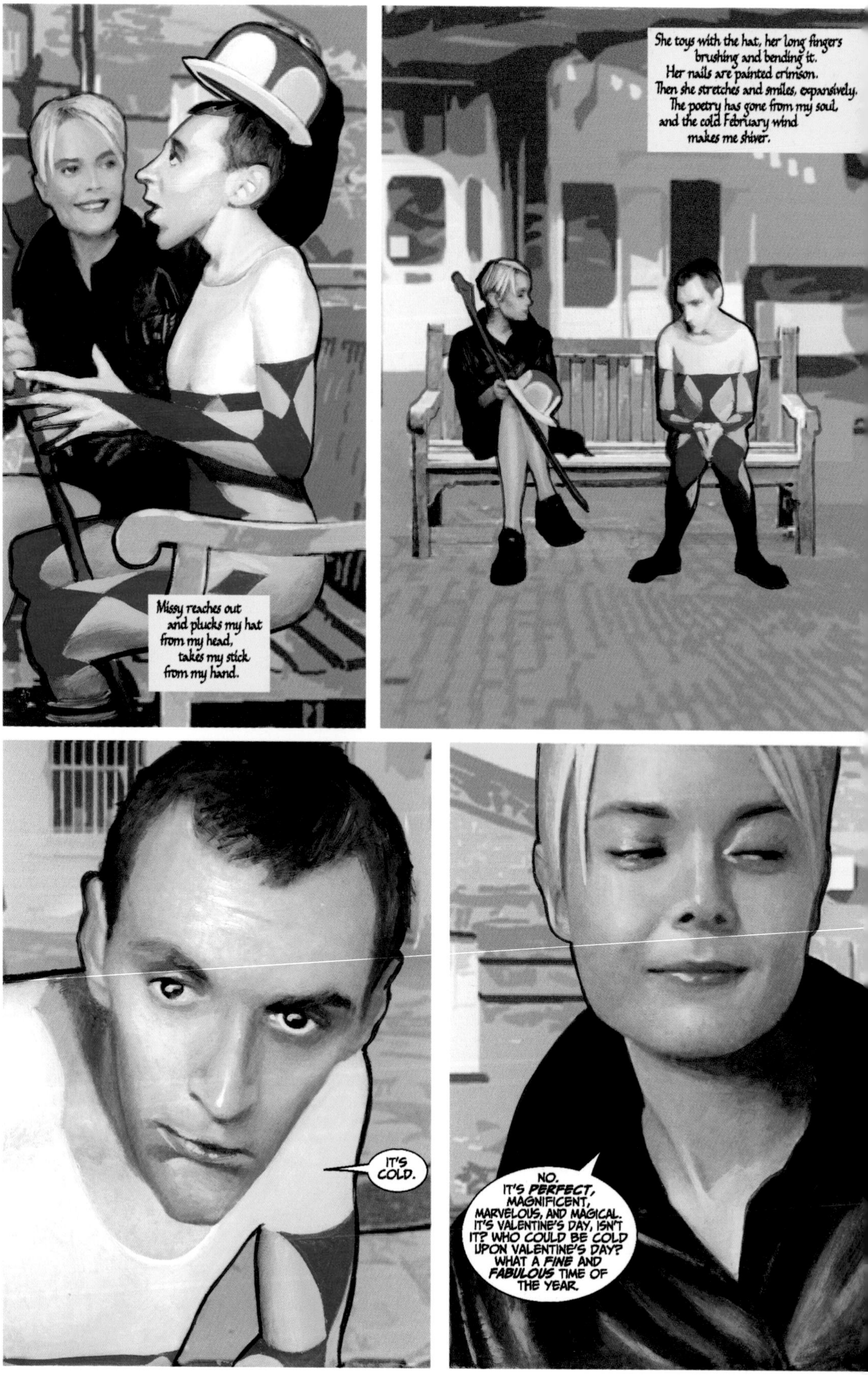
Missy reaches out
and plucks my hat
from my head,
takes my stick
from my hand.
She toys with the hat, her long fingers
brushing and bending it.
Her nails are painted crimson.
Then she stretches and smiles, expansively.
The poetry has gone from my soul,
and the cold February wind
makes me shiver.
IT'S COLD.
NO. IT'S PERFECT, MAGNIFICENT, MARVELOUS, AND MAGICAL. IT'S VALENTINE'S DAY, ISN'T IT? WHO COULD BE COLD UPON VALENTINE'S DAY? WHAT A FINE AND FABULOUS TIME OF THE YEAR.

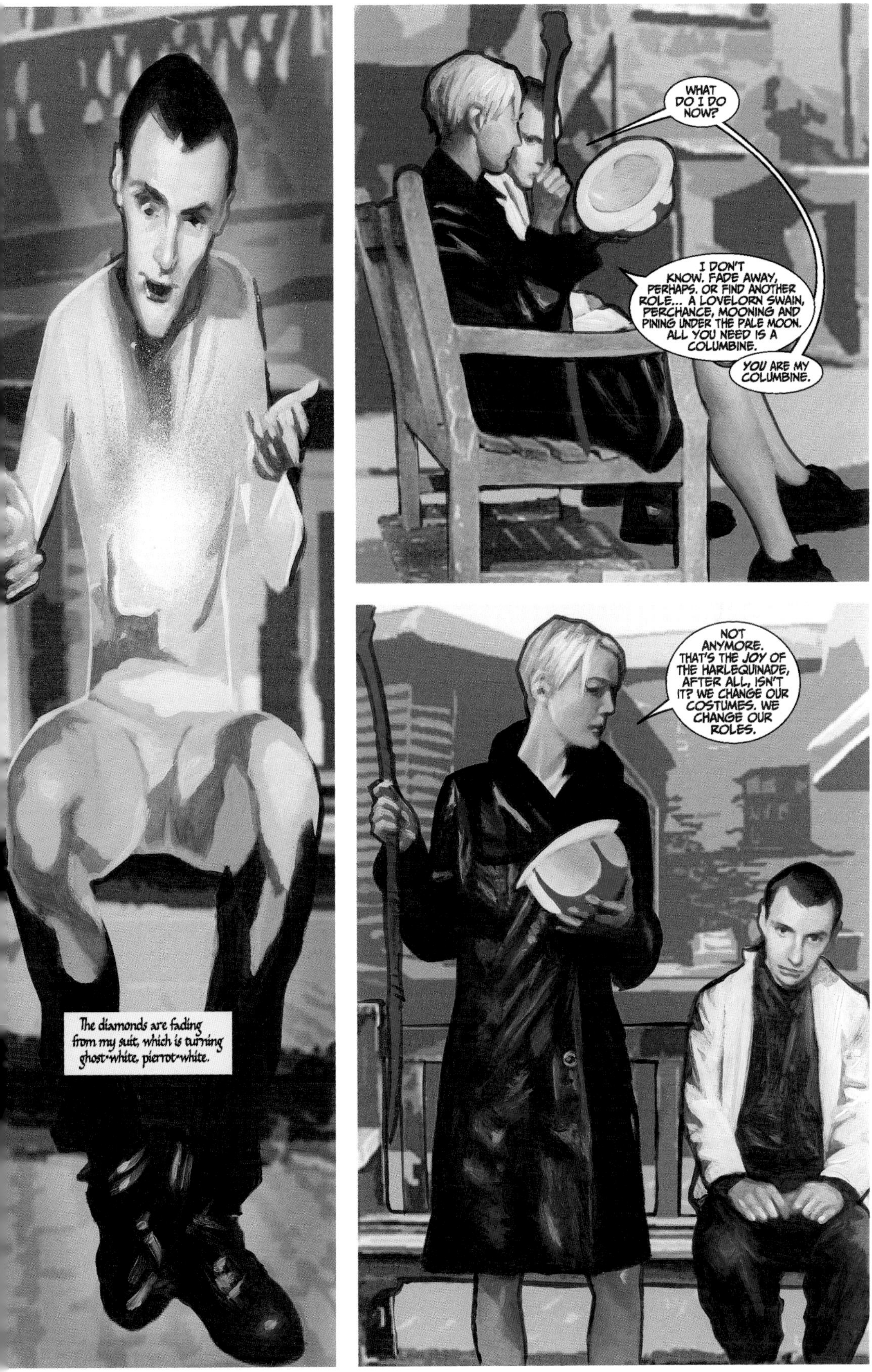
The diamonds are fading from my suit, which is turning ghost-white, pierrot-white.
WHAT DO I DO NOW?
I DON'T KNOW. FADE AWAY, PERHAPS. OR FIND ANOTHER ROLE... A LOVELORN SWAIN, PERCHANCE, MOONING AND PINING UNDER THE PALE MOON. ALL YOU NEED IS A COLUMBINE.
YOU ARE MY COLUMBINE.
NOT ANYMORE. THAT'S THE *JOY* OF THE HARLEQUINADE, AFTER ALL, ISN'T IT? WE CHANGE OUR COSTUMES. WE CHANGE OUR ROLES.

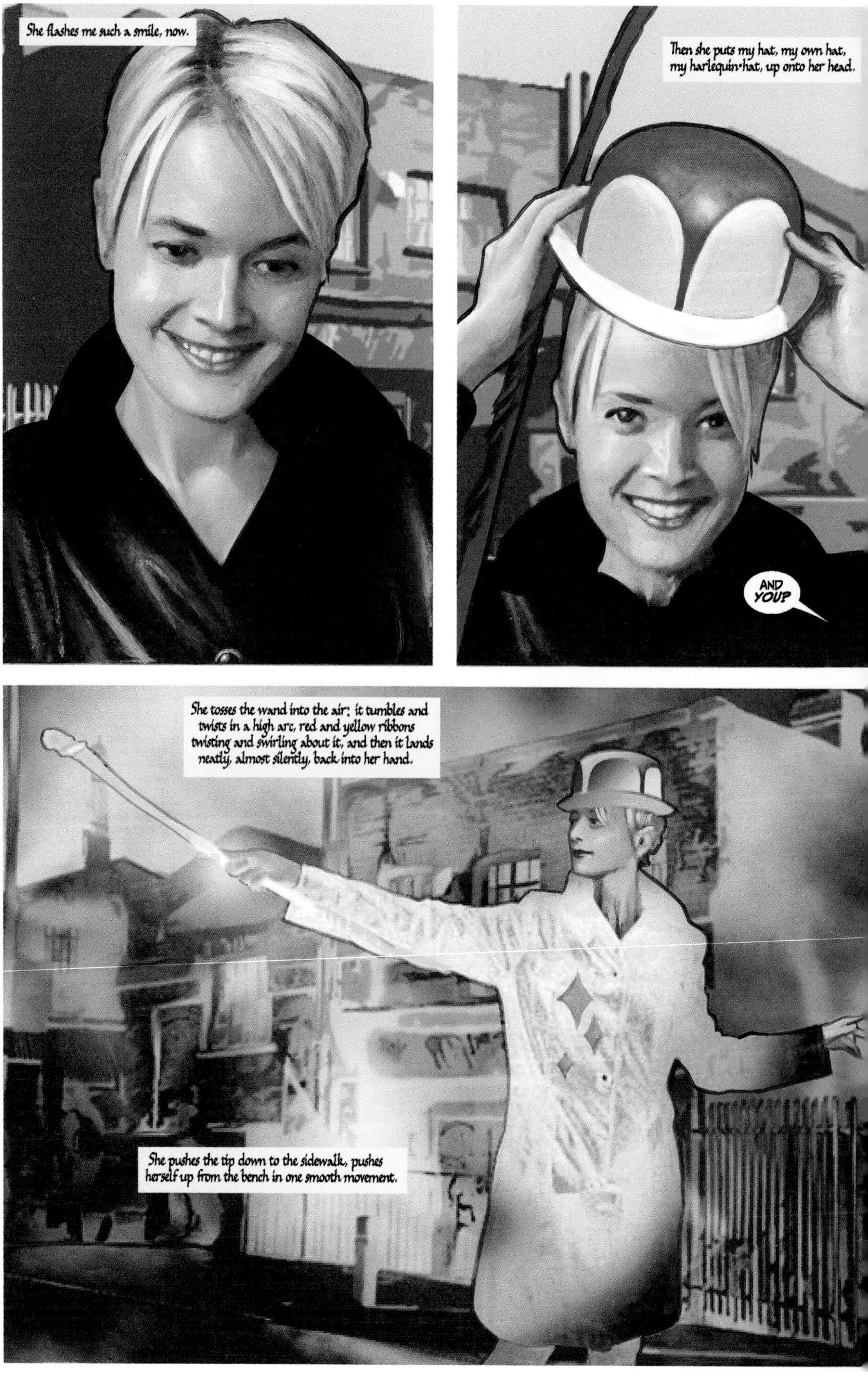
She flashes me such a smile, now.
Then she puts my hat, my own hat, my harlequin-hat, up onto her head.
AND YOU?
She tosses the wand into the air; it tumbles and twists in a high arc, red and yellow ribbons twisting and swirling about it, and then it lands neatly, almost silently, back into her hand.
She pushes the tip down to the sidewalk, pushes herself up from the bench in one smooth movement.

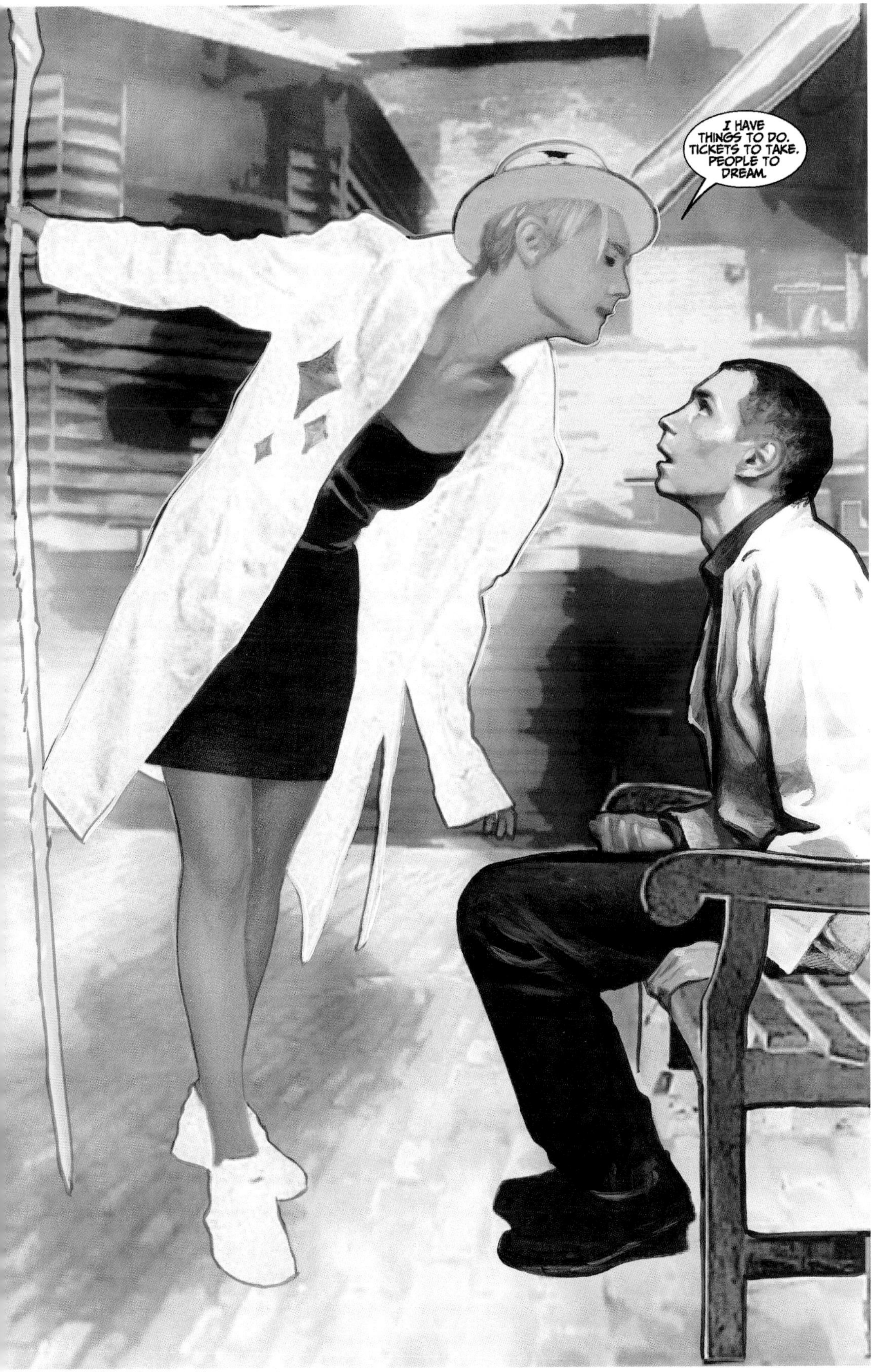
I HAVE THINGS TO DO. TICKETS TO TAKE. PEOPLE TO DREAM.

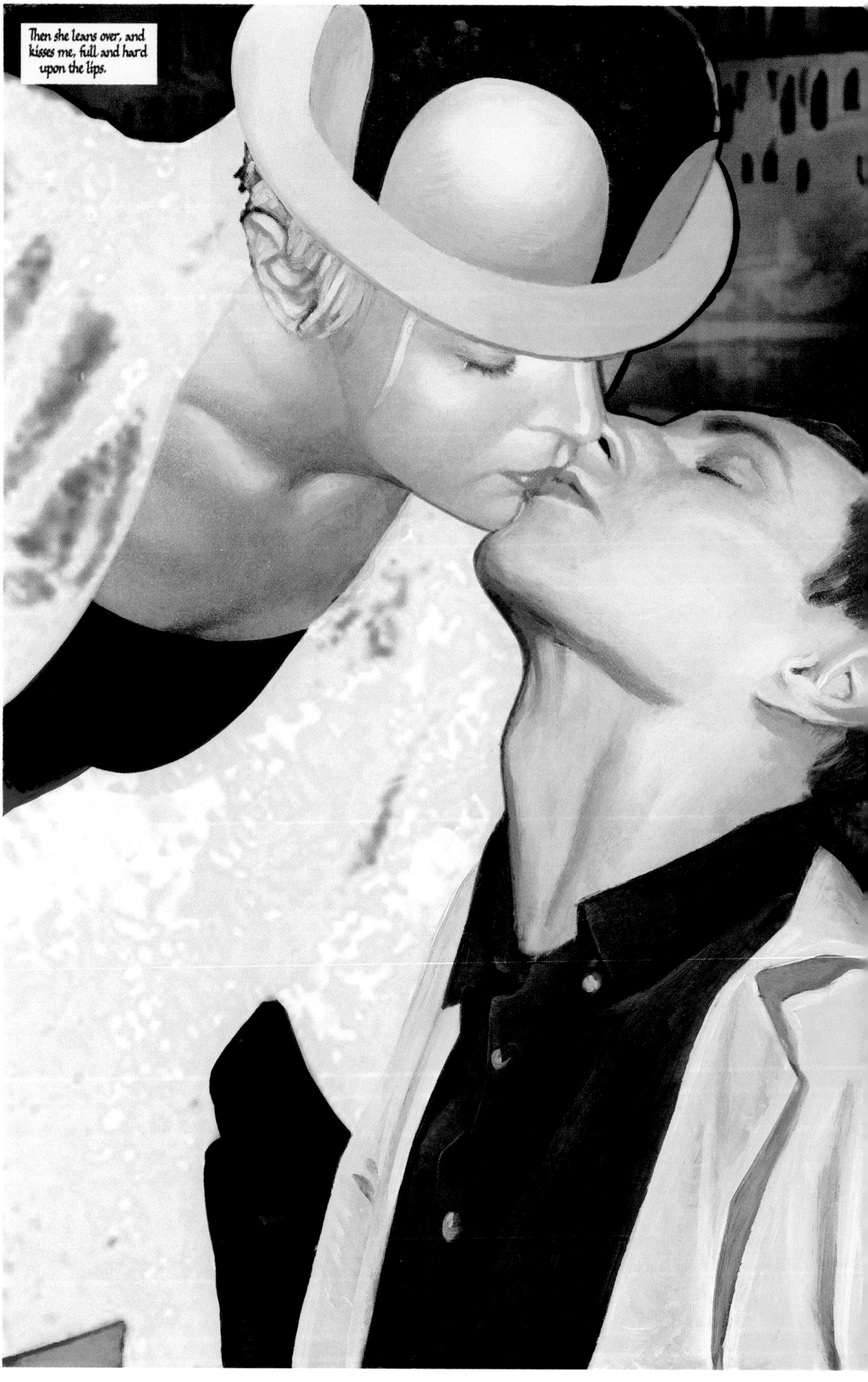
Then she leans over, and kisses me, full and hard upon the lips.

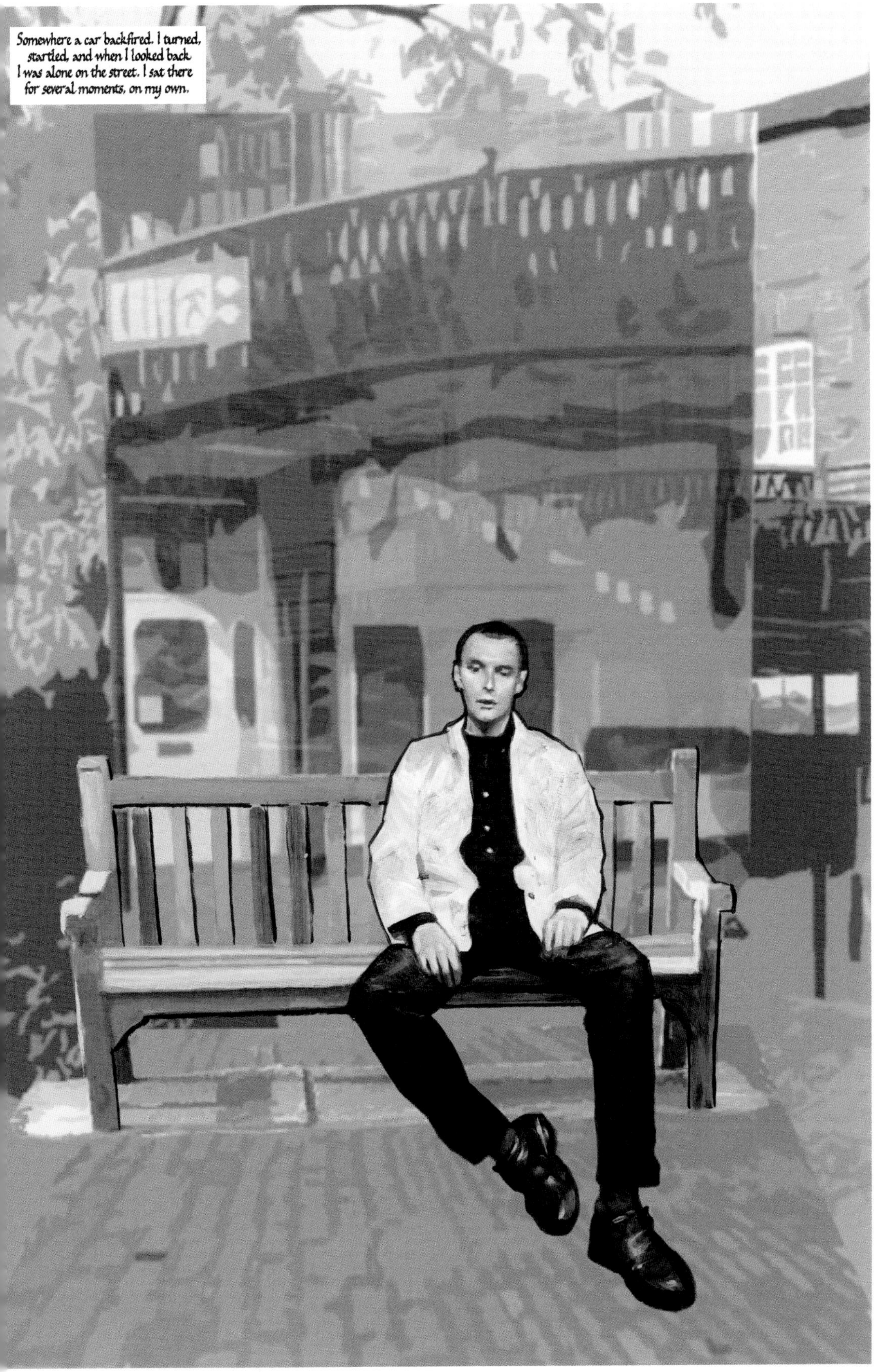
Somewhere a car backfired. I turned, startled, and when I looked back I was alone on the street. I sat there for several moments, on my own.

HEY, PETE. HAVE YOU FINISHED OUT THERE YET?

FINISHED? FINISHED WHAT, CHARLENE?

C'MON. HARVE SAYS YOUR CIGGIE BREAK IS OVER. AND YOU'LL *FREEZE*. BACK INTO THE KITCHEN.

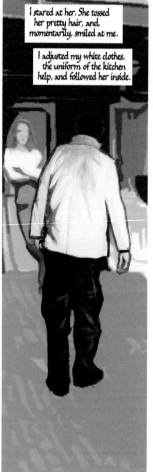

I stared at her. She tossed her pretty hair, and, momentarily, smiled at me.

I adjusted my white clothes, the uniform of the kitchen help, and followed her inside.

It's Valentine's Day, I thought. Tell her how you feel. Tell her what you think.

But I said nothing. I dared not. I simply followed her inside, a creature of mute longing.

Back in the kitchen a pile of plates was waiting for me; I began to scrape the leftovers into the pig-bin.

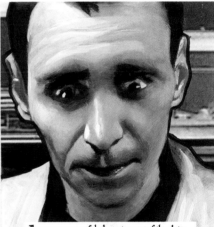

There was a scrap of dark meat on one of the plates, beside some half-finished ketchup-covered hash browns.

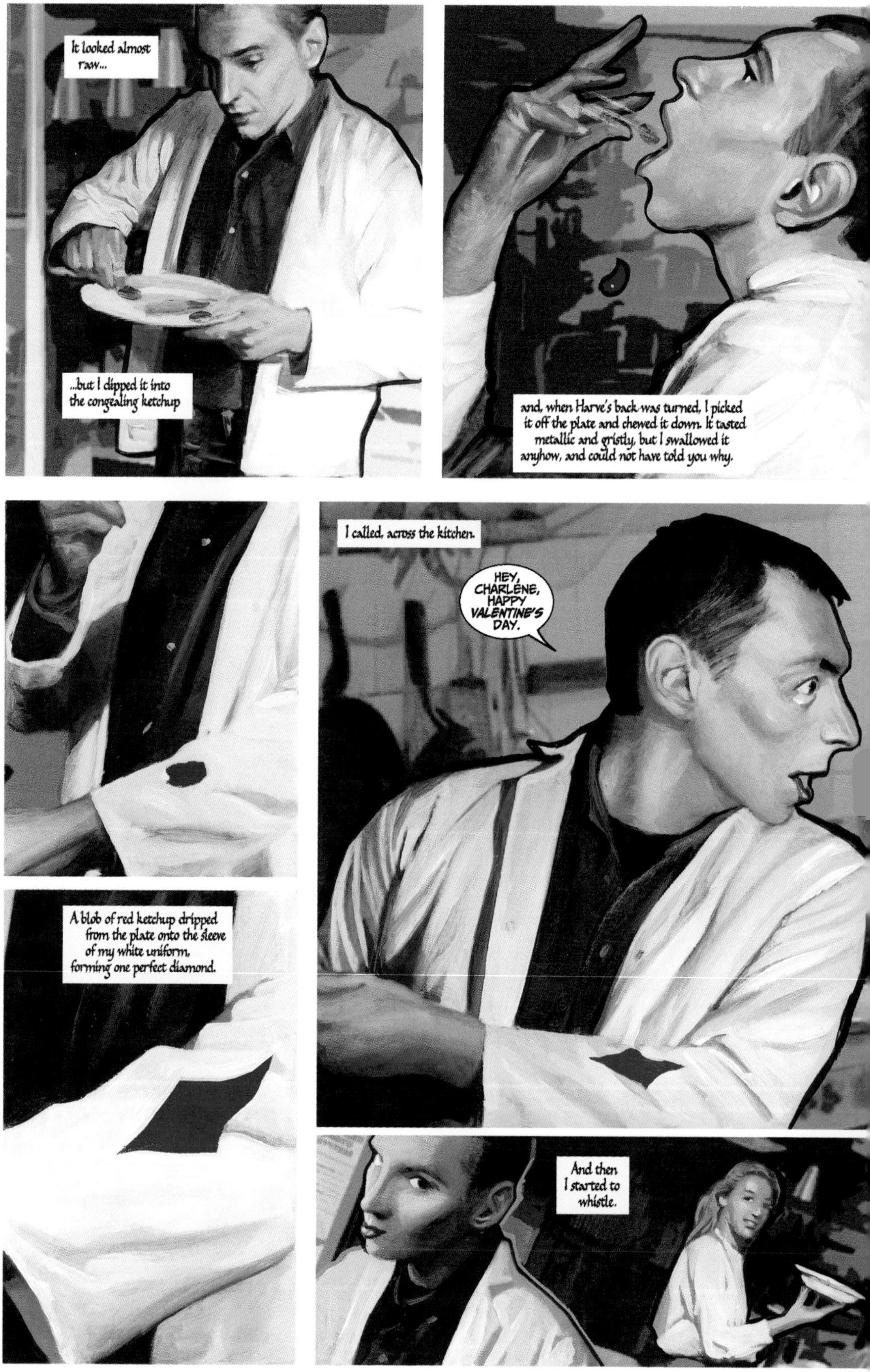
It looked almost raw...
...but I dipped it into the congealing ketchup
and, when Harve's back was turned, I picked it off the plate and chewed it down. It tasted metallic and gristly, but I swallowed it anyhow, and could not have told you why.
A blob of red ketchup dripped from the plate onto the sleeve of my white uniform, forming one perfect diamond.
I called, across the kitchen.
HEY, CHARLENE, HAPPY VALENTINE'S DAY.
And then I started to whistle.

NOTES ON A HARLEQUINADE

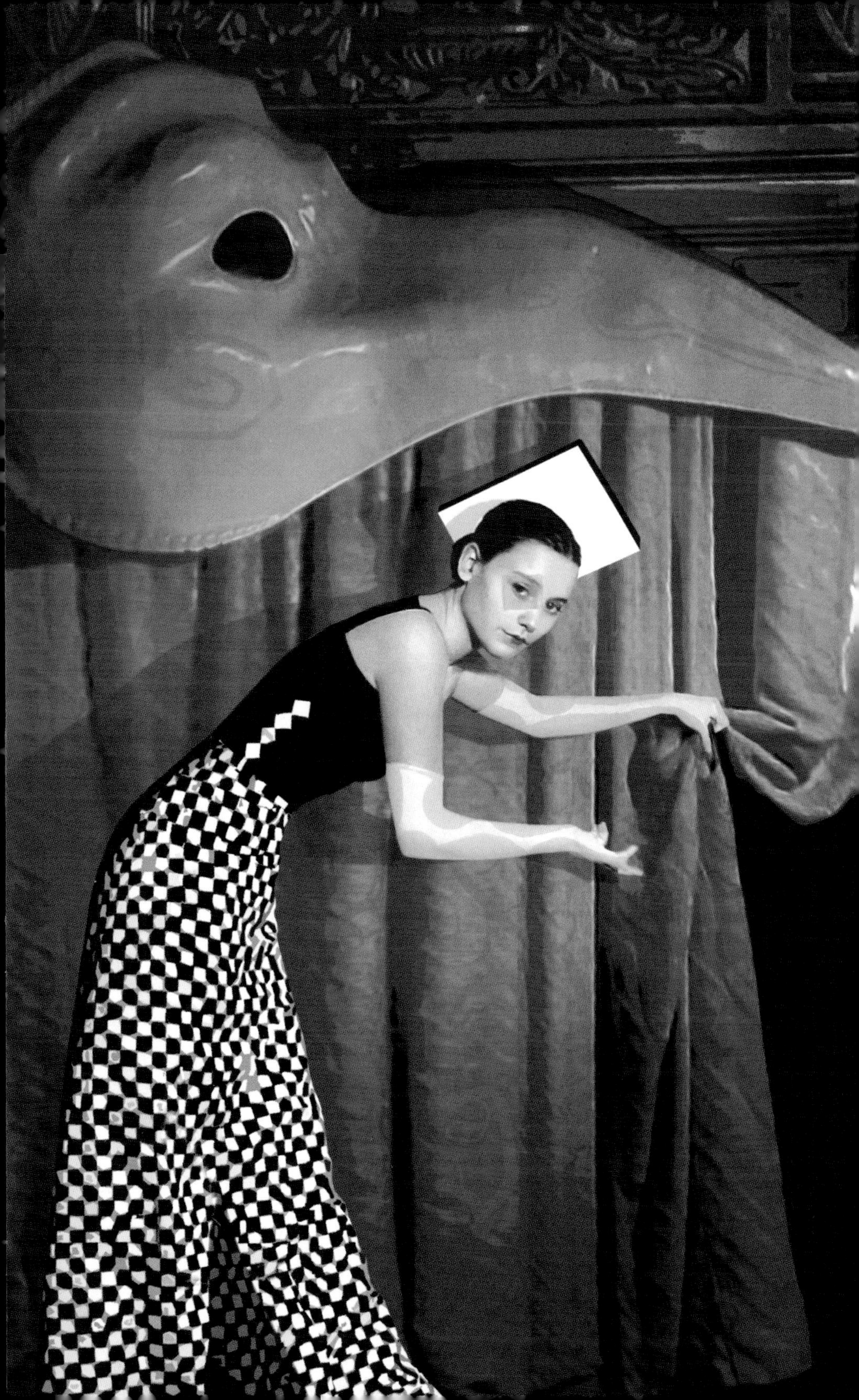

Harlequin (Har"le*quin) *n*. [F. *arlequin*, formerly written also *harlequin* prob. fr. OF. *hierlekin, hellequin*, goblin, elf, which is prob. of German or Dutch origin; cf. D. *hel* hell. Cf. Hell, Kin.] A buffoon, dressed in particolored clothes, who plays tricks, often without speaking, to divert the bystanders or an audience; a merry-andrew; originally, a droll rogue of Italian comedy.

*A*LL ROADS LEAD TO ROME, AND THIS ONE MAY START THERE, a couple of thousand years ago, with the popular farces known as the *Atellanae Fabulae*, or it may start with the Greeks, five hundred years before that, or earlier, with actors and performances lost to history. The roles of the sixteenth century Italian *Commedia dell'arte*, which became the French *vaudeville*, and, in the eighteenth and nineteenth centuries, the English Harlequinade, go back and go back. And Harlequin goes back further than most.

What would you like to know?

Who is Harlequin?

Harlequin was a stock character in the *Commedia dell'arte*; originally one of many stock characters (even if his roots went back further, deeper, and darker), he soon became one of the principal characters.

Harlequin arrived in England along with his contemporary, Mister Punch, after the Restoration, in the second half of the seventeenth century. By the early eighteenth century, Harlequin's name in the title of a play was already a box office draw — in 1723 the Harlequin Dr. Faustus was produced at Drury Lane, and Harlequin was a star, and the traditions of English Pantomime, and of the Harlequinade, had begun.

(E. Cobham Brewer, writing in his Guide to Phrase and Fable, over a hundred years ago, wrote: "*Harlequin*, in the British Pantomime, is a sprite supposed to be invisible to all eyes but those of his faithful Columbine. His office is to dance through the world and frustrate all the knavish tricks of the Clown, who is supposed to be in love with Columbine.")

Hang on a second here. Is there any difference between an English Pantomime and American Pantomime?

Sure. In America *Pantomime* is another word for mime, or what the English called "dumb-show" — acting without using words. In the British tradition, Pantomime is currently a form of theatrical entertainment popular at Christmas, in which traditional children's stories are acted out as broad comedies with a fixed cast of stock characters (which include the Dame — a grotesque woman played by a man — and the Principal Boy, always played by a leggy young woman). Songs are sung, slapstick is slapped and stuck, and there is often a transformation scene (as when Cinderella transforms from a kitchen girl to a princess).

In Victorian times, Pantomimes were Harlequinades, and all the dialogue was delivered in rhyming couplets.

By the 1930s the British Harlequin-based Pantomime tradition was in a severe decline; and I doubt a real Harlequinade has been produced as a Pantomime for fifty years, except as a curiosity.

These days "Pantos" have their own traditions, including that of casting minor television stars in leading roles.

Harlequin and Pierrot and Columbine went from the stage to the seaside, where Pierrot Shows (Pierrot, the white-faced clown, now topping the bill) were still performed at least until the onset of the Second World War.

And the Commedia dell'arte?

It translates, more or less, as the Comedy of Artisans or Craftsmen. It was a form of theatre without a script as such, but which relied on propelling a set of stock characters through an improvised series of variations on stock situations. Many of the characters had their own "bits" or *lazzi*, funny routines they worked into whatever they were performing.

Commedia dell'arte was performed masked, at least by the male actors, in the beginning, full-faced masks which shrank to half-masks as dialogue became more important, and shrank again as the *Commedia* became the Harlequinade, until the only characters who remained masked were the Harlequin, in his domino mask, and the Pierrot, who, while unmasked, was heavily powdered and worked in whiteface.

So who was Harlequin? And who were Pierrot, and Columbine, and the rest?

They were the stars. Actors playing them attained a certain amount of fame, or no fame at all, but the characters were all. Sometimes actors created versions of the characters who outlasted them. The characters of the *Commedia dell'arte* included:

Harlequin — originally, perhaps, just another one of the "zanies" — a lusty, funny, tricksy fellow. A creature of desire and lust.

By the time of the English Harlequinade, Harlequin had gained magical powers — invisibility, for one. His slap-stick, a noise-making stick, had become a magical staff.

In the earliest plays, his mask was black as soot.

Pantaloon — an elderly miser. If married, his wife is young and pretty, and cheats on him; otherwise he has daughters who need to be married off, but who will ignore his wishes as to the suitability of their suitors; or Pantaloon is in love with a village beauty, and will be disappointed. He is fated forever to be fooled.

The Doctor — a man of vast learning, who knows everything and understands nothing. There is no record of his ever curing anyone of any disease; Doctor, in the Italian, merely indicates a man of learning.

Pulcinella — the hunchbacked, hook-nosed, eccentric old curmudgeon, cruel and violent.

When he reached England, achieving fame a little after Harlequin, it was as a puppet, and a star in his own right: in his story, he kills his wife, first called Joan, then Judy, murders their baby, then sets off on his adventures, killing all who trouble him, until he kills the executioner sent to hang him and murders the devil himself. (Details of his life and crimes can be found in *Mister Punch*, a graphic novel by Messrs. Gaiman and McKean.)

The Captain — a braggart, a coward, a creature of lust and bravado, a brave appearance and a craven nature. He went by many names — Scaramouche was only one of them.

Pierrot — who began in the *Commedia dell'arte* as Pedrolino. When Harlequin plays tricks, Pierrot is the only one caught and punished. He dresses all in white, and his face is white as well. Sometimes he is mute. He loves, and longs, and wants. As the English

Harlequinade progressed Pierrot became more and more the Clown, but his love for Columbine remained unrequited.

Columbine — she went by many names, the Inamorata (or beloved): Isabella, Flaminia, Columbina, Silvia. Columbina, as she gained a distinct personality in the *Commedia,* became a serving girl, often working for Isabella, a witty, self-possessed young lady able to survive even the most involved intrigues.

As Columbine, in the Harlequinade, she became a simpler creature: a ballerina, or a beauty, loved by Pierrot, hopelessly, and by Harlequin, successfully.

The Lover — dapper, engaging, the lover has no character trait other than of being in love. He was Zeppo, in every Marx Brothers comedy. Or worse, he was all the guys who replaced Zeppo in the later Marx Brothers films.

How did the English Harlequinade differ from the Commedia dell'arte?

In the early Pantomime Harlequinade, the story would begin with a folk tale or fairy tale or popular story of the day, which led up to the transformation scene, in which, following a shadowy chase, the characters became the Harlequinade versions of themselves, and the hero would be revealed to the audience as Harlequin. But always there was a sense of archetypal characters performing a drama over and over, and of discovery, of who, in the Harlequinade, they truly were.

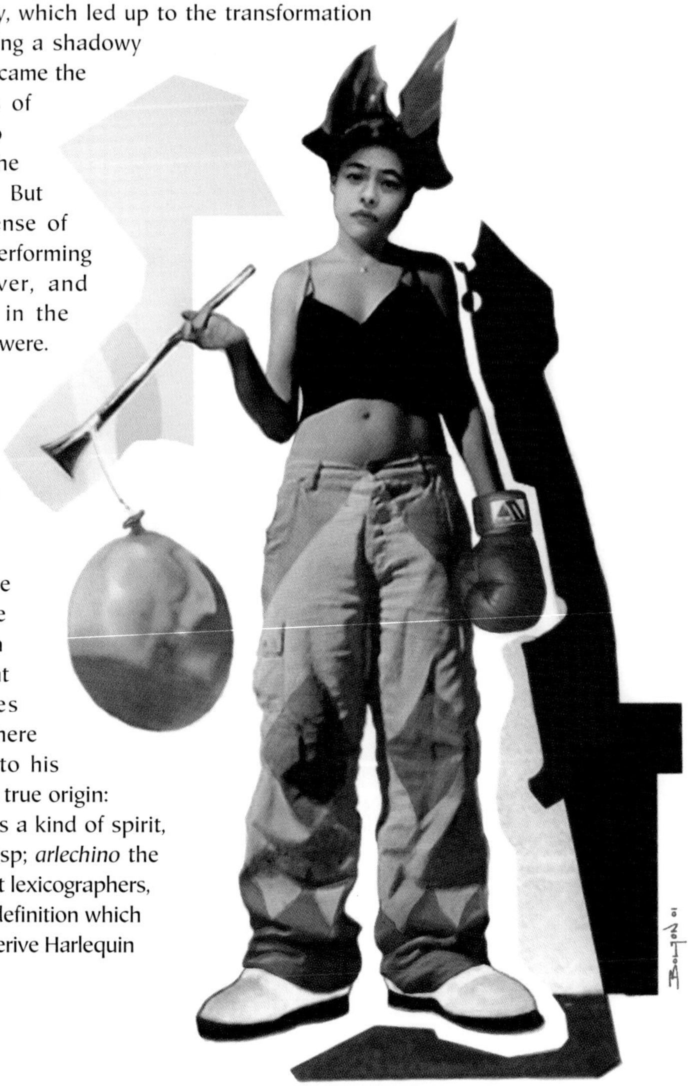
Bolton 01

And who was Harlequin?

That depends whom you believe.

There are those who trace Harlequin back to the *phallophores* in the Roman comedies, clutching giant phalluses, their faces blackened with soot. There are others who point to his name for clues as to his true origin: the French *herlequin* was a kind of spirit, a sprite, a will o' the wisp; *arlechino* the name of a devil; and most lexicographers, as you will see from the definition which prefaces this afterword, derive Harlequin straight from Hell ...

Neil Gaiman
August 15, 2001

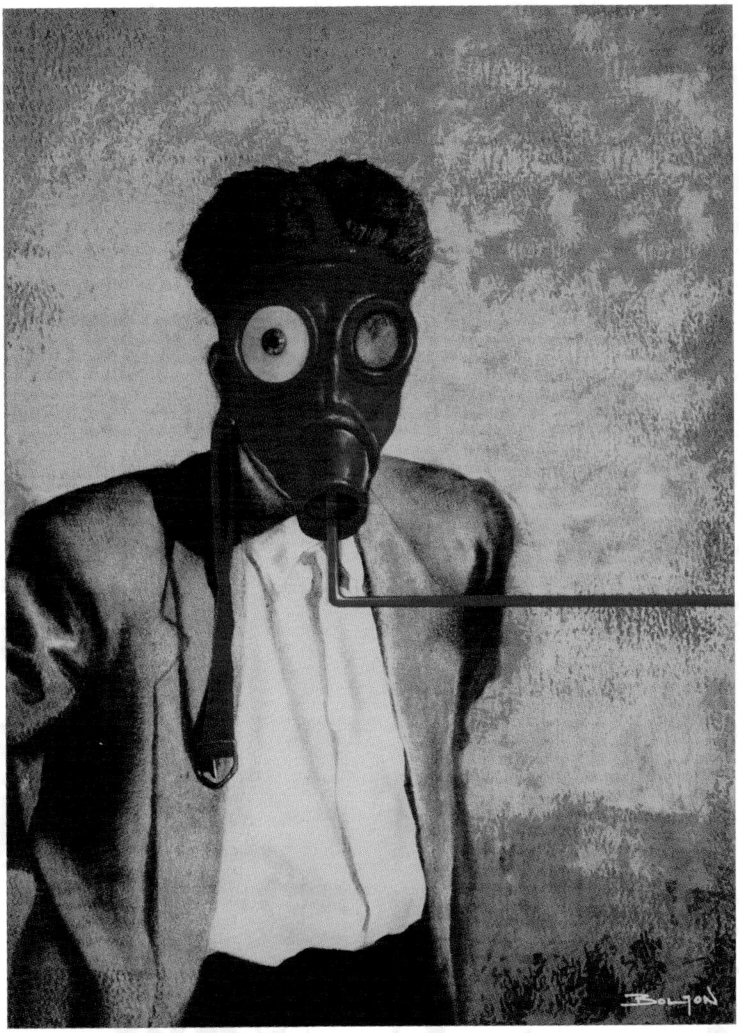
BOLTON

DRAWN IN DARKNESS

LATE IN THE AFTERNOON, JOHN MIRABILIS BOLTON PICKS UP HIS RED LEATHER GAS MASK AND WALKS DOWN THE PATH FROM HIS CROUCH END HOUSE TO THE CONVERTED BOMB SHELTER THAT SERVES HIM AS A STUDIO.

The gas mask, which has been blessed by the Pope, and the Dalai Lama, and the Supreme Sanguifex of the Clinical Brethren, is, Bolton claims, "essential to the process." If he is not wearing it, he cannot paint.

When asked whether it cuts down on his field of vision, Bolton smiles, slyly. "Only in reality," he explains. "I may lose vision, but I can see so much more with it on. It's shamanic, I suppose."

Bolton must be alone while he paints.

He starts each working day, he states, with no ideas whatsoever. "The subjects of the paintings need to come to me," he says, hesitantly. "You see, I have no imagination."

He is being precise here. The subjects of his paintings seek him out. They know where to find him. Bolton sits in his studio, grinding paints, preparing his blank canvases, all alone; when night falls he takes a taper and lights a few of the huge dark candles, melted now, if imagination amends them, into the shapes of fantastic beasts:

turtles and stonefish, dragons and demon-heads, and he waits to see whom, or what, he will be painting that night.

"The candles are my only superstition," says Bolton, who was made a Freeman and Servitor of Crouch End in the 1996 Honours List; if you encounter John Bolton within the bounds of Crouch End, you must remove your hat, and may not, by tradition, speak to him unless he speaks to you first. With the honour comes the right to cull the wild ermine, the small stoat-like beasts that plagued Crouch End long ago, when it was still a tiny village to the northwest of London, but have not been seen in the borough in living memory; even so, Bolton wears a traditional silver ermine knife at this belt. "When they return," he says, with a grin, "I'll be ready for them."

The subjects of his paintings come to him mostly at night. They slip through the shadows and walk down the gravestone steps to his studio, moonlight making their skin glow with a pale luminosity, candlelight glinting in their eyes and on the sharpness of their teeth.

Is he scared of them? The artist shakes his head. "They come to me," he explains. "The process — the making real — is as important to them as it is to me. They need me. Why would they hurt me?" But has he never been scared? He looks down. "You cannot let them see that you are afraid. Who would they find to paint them, if I were gone? Anyway," he adds, patting the silver ermine-skinner on his belt, "I have a knife."

Does he talk to them while he paints them? He does not answer. Instead he begins to light the candles.

How do they find out about him? Is there a grapevine among the naked and undead of London, a word passed along from pale vampire girl to restless satyr to faceless lamia? Bolton declines to speculate. "If they did not come to me, I would have nothing to paint," he says. "I am grateful, and leave it there."

What if he wished to paint something else? Fruit bowls or flowers? What then? He shivers, and shakes his head, and says nothing.

A yellow newspaper clipping, cut from a May 1965 copy of the *News of the World* and taped to the lichen-stained wall of his studio, tells of Bolton's tutelage in painting at the hands of an ancient madman who claimed to have been Richard Dadd, the Victorian painter and parricide, commonly believed to have died in 1886, seventy-five years to the day before Bolton was born. Bolton, however, refuses to discuss it. "It's water under the bridge," he says. "We must let the dead bury the dead. And I am grateful to all my teachers."

The sun is starting to set.

"You must leave now," says John Mirabilis Bolton, placing his red leather gas mask over his face, pulling the straps and buckles tight. "You would not want them to find you here." His voice is muffled, behind the leather and the glass. There are thirteen stone steps up from his studio to the mossy garden. In the trees at the bottom of the garden, something pale moves.

It is wisest not to look too closely.

— Neil Gaiman

NEIL GAIMAN

Born in 1781 in what is now known as Romania, Neil Gaiman, in later life librarian for the Margrave of Ghent, wrote several hundred books and stories in an obscure mixture of Polish and Latin. Unpublished during his lifetime, these manuscripts remained in a local museum until the 1930s, when they were smuggled to England, and were believed lost for good. In 1959, however, the manuscripts were discovered in a bread box in the attic of an abandoned hospital in Kettering, and were offered up for auction. Bought by an anonymous philanthropist, they were donated to the University of Lyme Regis. The "Gaiman translation" project began in 1964, and extracts

from the tales appeared initially in the Philological Digest (Volume 82, Winter 1970).

Commercially available translations of the stories, however, had to wait until 1989 and the ten volumes of *Sandman* (published in America by DC Comics). They have continued with such books as *Neverwhere*, *Stardust*, and the recently published *American Gods*.

Accusations of fraud and forgery have plagued the Gaiman manuscripts ever since their initial rediscovery, and it has recently been suggested that the stories were not, in fact, written by Gaiman but by another man, also in the employ of the Margrave of Ghent in the 1830s, of the same name.